Definitive Guide to Organic Lawn Care

DANIEL STOVER

My job is to maintain perfect grass.
I achieve that through organic practices.

CONTENTS

PREFACE

I want to take a moment to congratulate you on taking the first step in creating a custom organic solution in order to grow and maintain your lawn. By gaining the knowledge shared within these pages you will be creating a superior solution to what any chemical lawn care company can provide you. It doesn't matter if you're a homeowner or a landscaping professional, after reading this guide you will have learned the exact steps needed to become an expert on organic lawn care. In this no fluff guide I have given you everything you need and nothing you don't in order to get you up to speed as fast as possible.

My name is Daniel Stover, a GCSAA golf course superintendent with over 20 years of experience in the organic turf field. Through these years I have tested countless organic products and methods to help my golf courses perform at the highest level. These practices have helped me revive chemically abused soils, combat insects, ward off diseases and wipe out nematodes. The golf courses I have built and maintained range from the cold north east of New England to the hot and arid southern Caribbean. My courses have hosted televised PGA Tour tournaments, received Golf Week's top 50 in North America, Golf Advisor's #1 for course conditions in the United States and USA Today's Best Course in the Caribbean. The diversity of environmental conditions and variety of turf species I have maintained allow me to help you no matter where you are in the world or the type of grass you grow.

The approach I have slowly learned over my career is that a healthy plant does not need chemicals. It's a simple philosophy but it has allowed me to gain a huge advantage over my competition. While most of my industry focuses on reacting to plant problems with chemicals, I rely on creating natural balances within the soil to fight any problems that my grass may encounter. The secret to achieve that perfectly healthy grass and natural balance is an active microbial population housed within a well-drained growing medium. Now, I realize that the thought of learning soil microbiology may seem rather daunting but I promise you it is very simple. You will quickly learn how this one two punch is a powerful symbiotic relationship that will work for you to grow a dense root system. This root system will be the foundation needed to grow green grass.

This knowledge on soil microbiology was never something I was taught through my career mentors and rarely discussed when I was in school. It came through endless research and trial and error of products and methods in order to shed light on what exactly what works the best. Within the turf business we are bombarded with knowledge from peers, steered by fertilizer salesman and distracted by marketing of products that simply don't work. For these reasons I needed to get myself focused on testing of organic products that I thought had merit and could help me reach my goals. The idea was to do what nobody else was doing in my field and become that much better than my competition. In order to take that first step I needed to start a detailed journal. Products, cultural practices, mowing patterns, heights, watering and everything in between, I kept track of everything. This documentation made quick work of sifting out the snake oil products from the all-stars. To this day I still am constantly testing out new methods and products on my courses. That freedom to test out methods and products on a daily basis within hundreds of acres of grass allows me to find the very best of what works at an extremely fast pace. Not only is this testing paramount to keep me on the cutting edge but it allows me to quickly report back to my readers.

One of the great motivators for me to get this guide started was the fact that there were a lot of hobbyists, gardeners and television personalities who write lawn care books but very few actual turf professionals who do. I am sure that there are a lot of people that can write a book about lawn care and deliver a few good pointers. But I am in the business of creating custom solutions to keep grass the healthiest it can be for decades. That's my whole career; growing green grass and training others how to do so. I go to work to maintain grass ranging from 0.100" - 3.75". There are no other professions that can do that. No matter the environment the grass grows in my career relies on my ability to grow flawless turf and that's what I am here to teach you how to do.

If you are growing a new lawn or maintaining an old one there is no topic left out. Everything in this guide ties together toward the goal of getting your soil to do most of the work for you. It's important to keep in mind that without sound fertilization, watering, mowing and cultivation techniques your lawn will never be as good as it can be. This guide will walk you through every step of the way and show you how everything works in harmony to create a truly sustainable solution.

I strive to make this guide as complete as possible to cover all your lawn care maintenance needs. I update this book multiple times per year with information from the latest studies and what is working for me on my golf courses. However, I realize that to be a complete guide just one book cannot cover every problem that may arise. For that reason, check the back of the book to find out how to get more help from me, Daniel Stover.

TURF TYPES

Cool season grasses

Grass types considered "cool season" are the blue grasses, rye grasses, fescues and bent grasses. Most often cool season grass seeds (excluding bent grass) will be packaged as a mix for different situations such as sun, shade and or high traffic areas.

With the exception of Bentgrass you should be mowing no lower than 3". Keeping the grass tall will help promote deep rooting, help shade out weeds and provide the plant with more leaf tissue to aide in photosynthesis. As a general rule: the taller the grass the deeper the green.

In the United States these grass types are often used in New England, the Upper Midwest, the High Plains, and Northern California up to the Pacific Northwest. These regions include zones 1-7 (USDA Planting zone map). In transitional zones cool season grasses are also used to "over-seed" the dormant warm season grass to keep a green look throughout the winter months.

Kentucky bluegrass - A fine and tightly knit dark green grass, it is often mixed with other species for best results. It is popular throughout the northern and transition zones for its ability to grow in shady conditions. I like a mowing height of 3.5" in most situations. Pay attention to the label while buying Kentucky bluegrass seed and make sure it does not contain annual bluegrass. This variety of bluegrass is a weed and will be hard to remove from your lawn without the use of chemical treatments.

Perennial Ryegrass - Found primarily in the northern and transition zones and needs full sun to thrive. Perennial Ryegrass has a medium texture and grows in clumps or bunches but is often blended with fescues and bluegrass for a uniform look and feel. Because of its fast growth it is often used to over-seed a dormant lawn in the south, giving the homeowner a green lawn year round. Mow at a height of 3.5". Don't be tempted to save money by getting Annual ryegrass, it is much rougher and much less attractive.

Fine Fescue - An excellent performer in shade and cold, this is often added to fill in where other cool season species fail. It has three varieties; creeping red fescue, hard fescue and chewing's fescue. A heat wave of more than a week, could require more care and watering, as high temps are stressful for this species. Fine fescue a good choice for high traffic areas and can handle most soil conditions and climates. Mow at a height of 3.5".

Tall Fescue - Due to its adaptability, quick germination, and low maintenance Tall Fescue is usually found in mixes containing other species. Tall Fescue has a coarse texture that grows in shade loving dense clumps. Tall fescue is extremely wear tolerant and is popular on sports fields and other high traffic lawns. Mow at the height of 3.5".

Bentgrass – This grass is typically used for tennis courts, outdoor bowling, golf courses and high end residential lawns and not recommended for organic lawns. The skill and expense needed to maintain this species usually eliminates it as a possible home lawn turf. It requires more watering, mowing, aerating, dethatching and more fertilizers than other cool season grass varieties. It is adapted to cool, humid regions and prefers sunny areas but will tolerate some shade. It tolerates low temperatures but will discolor early in the fall. Despite what anyone tells you do not use this grass as an over seeding candidate. Its aggressive growth characteristics and persistence during summer months make it near impossible to fully eradicate. If however you are seeking to grow this grass for a grass tennis court or croquet court you will need a reel mower and maintain at 0.185"- 0.225".

My suggestion - Use a cool season grass mix of endophyte enhanced varieties. You can buy pre-packed seed designed for the environment you are growing in such as shade, full sun or compaction. The endophyte enhancements will help minimize the damage from diseases and insects.

Warm season grasses

Warm-Season grasses are of a warm climate origin and thrive during the summer months. They are tough and form a dense lawn cover that thickens as they age. As fall weather temperatures drop leaves turn brown and won't green up again until warm weather returns. Depending on where you live in general they are green a little over half the year.

Growing and maintaining a good-looking warm season grass is more involved than a cool season grass. Choosing grass varieties is trickier in some circumstances. There is much higher thatch layer (a layer of dead, dying and diseased material created by grass during its natural growth process) accumulation and thus heavier cultivation practices are needed to maintain a healthy lawn. Where winter mowing heights are listed below some species should be scalped in the summer months along with an aggressive verticut. More on this within the cultivation chapter.

In the United States warm-season grasses are best suited for southern regions. These regions include zones 7-13 (USDA Planting zone map). Within these zones there are six species of warm season turf that you should become aware of before choosing a grass type for your lawn. Deciding which grass is best depends on your preferences and situation.

Bermuda grass – A dark green fine textured grass. It has good cold tolerance but it does not do well in the shade unless you plan on using the TifGrand variety. It also has great wear tolerance and can withstand very low mowing heights. I recommend a mowing height of 2" and despite what anybody tells you do not use any of the seeded varieties. Seeded varieties lack the color, density and appearance of the sprig or sod varieties. I recommend *Celebration* as a sprigged or sodded variety.

One thing to note is that this is an aggressive grass and requires more work than others. This grass should be scalped to the height of 1-1.5" during the summer months and verticut aggressively to reduce thatch. Once maintained at the desired summer height for 1-2 months you may begin raising the height of the grass to its 2" goal. This will help keep looking thick and even during the winter months.

Centipede - A medium textured grass with light green color. Its cold tolerance is slightly lower than Bermuda grass and should not be used in high traffic areas. Mowing heights of 3" will suffice. Shade tolerance is better than Bermuda but less shade tolerant then St. Augustine or Zoysia. It's not the prettiest grass because of its light green color. I would consider using another grass that fits your situation.

Saint Augustine – A coarse textured grass with poor cold tolerance. This species doesn't stand up well to heavy traffic. In the United States this grass is most prevalent in Florida. In my opinion the texture of the grass on bare feet is a deal breaker. It has good shade tolerance but Zoysia can do just as well in the same situations and look better doing so. Mow at a height of 3.5 - 3.75".

Kikuyu grass – A coarse-textured, light green grass, sometimes mistaken for St. Augustine grass. In the United States this grass is more common on the west coast and is rarely used on the east. It's hard to recommend this grass for a home lawn situation because of its aggressive growth habits. It is extremely hard to confine in a given space and can quickly spread into undesirable areas. This grass is most common within California. Mowing heights should be 1.5-2".

Zoysia - A fine to medium texture with good cold tolerance. Often times this grass is mistaken for Bermuda grass but has slightly brighter green color. Like Bermuda it doesn't handle shade too well. If your lawn does not have heavy foot traffic this may be the grass of choice for you. My choice here is either the Empire or Emerald variety. Mow at a 2-2.5" height.

Sea Shore Paspalum – A fine textured grass with very poor cold tolerance. Only plant this species if you are in zone 9b-13. This grass has the most salt tolerance out of any species and has a similar wear tolerance of Bermuda. It has a strikingly bright green color and has acceptable shade tolerance. It can tolerate mowing height from medium to extremely short. I suggest mowing at 1.75" for home lawn purposes. If you live directly on the sea shore and are willing to put in the extra effort than this could be the perfect grass for you. I like the Sea Dwarf, Supreme and Platinum varieties but they come in sprig form only. There are seeded varieties also available like sea spray and dynasty which may prove to be an easier solution for you.

Much like Bermuda grass it's important to follow heavy cultivation practices for the summer months. Scalping to the height of 1" and verticutting during the summer will be needed. Maintain the height of 1" for several months during the hottest part of the season.

My suggestion –The grass you choose in a warm climate has to do with how much maintenance you would like to perform, what your seasonal temperatures are like, texture and color preferences.

For relatively easy maintenance Centipede or St. Augustine would suffice for most warm season climates. St. Augustine works better in sub tropic regions where Centipede works better on the cooler side of the spectrum. The problem with both species is they might not be aesthetically pleasing enough for you and have extremely coarse texture. For grasses that catch the eye one would plant a Zoysia grass variety or Sea Shore Paspalum if you live in a year round very warm climate. In most situations I would not suggest Bermuda grass for a homeowner situation as it's not a particularly pretty looking grass and most varieties do not work well in shade.

GRASSING

Seeding

Establishing a lawn from seed (or sprigs) is the best and least expensive method to growing in a new lawn. Purchasing the proper lawn seed is quite simple, but there are a few things you need to look for.

First you want to make sure that the seed you're purchasing has not been sitting on the shelf for more than a year unless it is sealed properly in a plastic tub or bucket. What I mean by sealed is don't use seed in open barrels from which you would scoop the seed out and weigh it. These barrels can be exposed to the air for several months to years without proper sealing. This storage method lowers the quality of the seed and lowers germination (growing from seed to a plant) rates. Its best to look for seed with endophyte enhancements. This will reduce insect and disease problems down the road and prove to be worth the extra few dollars spent.

The best time to spread your seed depends on the type of grass you're establishing. Generally for cool season grasses I suggest seeding in the spring. At the time the soil temperatures are warm enough to germinate your seed and grow before the hot summer months. Also this will give the plant plenty of time to grow and become fully established before winter.

If you have chosen to seed a warm season variety grass then I would do so in the late spring. This will be warm enough to germinate the seed and with summer right around the corner a quick grow in should not be a problem.

Equipment

The first step in any grow in from seed is the proper equipment. You can get away with just about any type of spreader to spread your seed but there are a few things you need to know before a purchase. There are two types of spreaders with upsides and downsides to both. In the name of keeping this an inexpensive purchase you can buy one spreader for both fertilizer and seeding applications. Before purchasing a type of spreader make sure you review the fertilization section to get a sense of calibration and application requirements of both spreader types.

Drop spreader

Pros:

Accurate

No wasted product

Spreading not influenced by wind

Cons:

Spreading takes longer

Harder to spread fertilizer

Requires the use of marking flags for accuracy

My suggestion – If you have a larger lawn a drop spreader is probably not the choice for you. These spreaders require accurate application and the larger the lawn the more skill and time is required to apply correctly. Where drop spreaders can spread two to three feet for expensive models, rotary spreaders can spread ten feet or more and require less accuracy. If you have a small lawn with a lot of plant beds to avoid, then a drop spreader may be the best choice for you.

Rotary spreaders

Pros:
Quick applications
Requires less accuracy

Cons:
Influenced by wind
Harder to avoid wasted product

My suggestion - If you have a larger lawn or want a spreader where you can get jobs done fast then rotary would be your best option. At most you can spend upwards of $500-$700 for an excellent spreader such as an Andersons or Lesco. However for quite a bit cheaper you can find a decent rotary spreader on amazon for around $100.

Preparation

The first and foremost thing you should always do before preparation of a home lawn is to take soil samples. These can be fairly inexpensively and will provide you with recommendations on what you should apply to your soil before seeding. This process takes a few weeks to get results back, but taking soil samples is vital in making decisions on what exactly to apply. Your local university does soil tests for cheap. For a more comprehensive package visit definitiveguidetoorganiclawncare.com and find my soil testing options. To learn exactly how to go about taking samples please find the soil samples section under the fertilization chapter.

Most seed companies suggest to till your seed area before seed application. This is something you can forego but just keep in mind that skipping this step will be a gamble with creating good seed to soil contact. Tilling in preparation for seed is definitely going to give the best results as it will give seeds a soft surface for new roots to penetrate, provide the necessary oxygen, relieve compaction and increase microbial activity.

To save you a lot of headaches in the future you need to first kill all the weeds before seeding. A simple solution of vinegar and a teaspoon or two of dish soap mixed in a small sprayer will kill just about any weed you have. You may want to spray once and make sure your weeds are dead in a week or two. If they are not dead spray them again. The second spray will be the nail in the coffin and you will be able to seed your lawn within the next week after your second spray. The acid in the vinegar is harmful to plants, so be sure to wait at least a few days after all plants have died before you spread grass seed. With the addition of soil tilling this amount of time should have given your soil microbes to break down the vinegar into a non-harmful form. Do not attempt to kill weeds with a tilling machine. This will just end up spreading new weed seeds throughout your lawn.

Once all weeds are dead and you wish to till your lawn the best results are tilling to a depth of 4". Most tillers can be rented per day for under $50. Tilling is also something that want to not overdo. Don't go over your lawn two times. Don't bother breaking up large clumps. Large clumps are often held together by organic debris. This debris should not be over tilled as it can be detrimental to your soil structure.

After tilling you should then apply your needed soil amendments at the recommended rates via the advice of your soil tests. If you are unable to conduct soil testing you can apply gypsum at the rate of 10-20lbs of product per 1000sqft. Gypsum (commonly called calcium sulfate) is safe for all plants and is a natural product made of calcium and sulfur. An important thing to look for on the bag is to make sure this is not the dihydrate type of gypsum ($CaSO_4*2H_2O$). These can be labeled as "gypsum equivalents" but extensive testing has shown these products and are not equivalent at all and can take years to break down in the soil. These products will not help you alleviate soil problems. Real gypsum (calcium sulfate anhydrate $CaSO_4$) will help you flush built up salts, correct magnesium and calcium imbalances and further aerate your soil structure.

After your products have been applied then you can rake the top of your soil to smooth the surface and work in your soil amendments. Once these products have been applied and raked in you are then ready to apply your seed.

Application

For a professional application I would suggest to calibrate your spreader to the rate suggested on the bag. Never go by spreader settings found on the bag, these numbers can be way off and only should be used as a starting point for calibration purposes. This application rate can be anywhere from 1/2lb to 1.5lbs per 1000sqft. Lean on the heavy side for a quicker and fuller appearance. I than usually take my chosen rate and cut it in half and spread in two different directions (two directions at half rate means a completed full rate) to assure even coverage, avoid skips and hide overlap. Please see our calibration section within the fertilization chapter for more info on calibration and application.

For people who have opted to go with rotary spreaders remember that seeds will inevitably make it into your undesirable areas. A day of either spraying vinegar or pulling grass seedlings out of plant beds may be in your future.

Fertilization

Once your seed has been fully spread, its time to put down a starter fertilizer. Go with a fertilizer based off from your soil testing recommendations. This fertilizer should also have a slow release organic form of nitrogen. If you do not yet have your soil recommendations back yet you can plan on putting down 1/2lb of nitrogen(N) , 1/2lb of phosphorus(P) and also 1/2lb of potassium(K) (see our calibration section for more details) with the added benefits of micronutrients such as iron and manganese. A good complete fertilizer I use on my golf courses is Nature Safe 5-6-6. A more readily available product would be Dr. Earths 4-4-4.

Rolling

At this point in time many landscapers will tell you to rake in your seed. I normally however do not bother. I find this to be a counterproductive process as you have spent time assuring uniform coverage. Raking in seed would only create areas of thick and thin grass. What I suggest to use instead is a water filled lawn roller it in order to get good seed to soil contact. These rollers can be found on amazon for relatively cheap. A good alternative is to roll over it with lawn mower tires (if your lawn is small enough). Rolling over new grass seed will not hurt the seed and will help with seed to soil contact. Once rolling has been completed its time to cover your seeds to protect them from the hot sun, birds and erosion from rain.

Top dressing

There are a few ways to properly top dress your newly applied grass seed. One is sand and one is straw. Straw can be used on both warm season and cool season but really works best on cool season grasses. The reason being is that warm season grasses spread laterally fast due to their stolons and rhizomes. Straw will only slow the development of a thick lush canopy. The major benefit to straw is that it's cheap and quick to spread. When you do elect to use straw as your seed topdressing do not use hay. The difference between straw and hay is that hay has been cultivated when the plant is still green causing molds and mildew to thrive within the hay bail. It not only makes things messy to spread, it can spread unwanted fungus to your grass. Straw is cultivated when the plant is dormant and brown, no mess, no mildew, no fungus.

Spread the straw over your grass by hand, with just enough to cover the ground so you cannot see the soil. It's not an exact science but too much and you risk sunlight not being able to hit the seedlings and too little and your risk your seeds drying out.

Sand is the only alternative I can get behind and really in many ways it's a superior topdressing choice to protect your seed. The problem is that its labor intensive and much more expensive. It also is a bit more technical as you need to know exactly what type of sand you are using. Construction sand is not an ideal sand to use because of its nature to bind to each other leaving very little pore space between the particles. Then you have to know what sand particle size you need due to your soil sample results. A good rule of thumb here is to use coarse topdressing sand no matter your soil test results. A quick google search of local topdressing sand plants will come up with something but keep in mind a truck load of sand may cost you upwards of $700. The goal is ¼-1/2" of topdressing sand over your entire seeded area. A rule of thumb is that 14 cubic yard dump truck should cover a 10,000 sqft lawn with about ½" of sand.

Watering

With the first watering after your straw has been applied make sure to wet the soil to the point of saturation. This amount of time can vary depending on your soil type and what sprinkler you are using. With whatever method you are watering be sure to water gently to assure seeds do not move around. Watering may take up to an hour with several breaks in between to avoid puddling to initially saturate the soil. After that you can get away with light watering or just enough to keep the top 1/2inch of the soil moist.

It is a good idea to check soil moisture with your finger to gauge how many times a day you should be watering (check the soil moisture, not the straw moisture). In most situations a watering during the morning and a watering during the heat of the day will suffice. Check every couple of hours at first to get a gauge on watering schedule. The same goes for how many minutes a day you can water. Puddling is something you want to avoid, and so is a dry top layer. I wish I could give you an exact timing of all circumstances but this differs in all areas. In colder climates on a cloudy day you may be able to get away with one watering per day. Adversely on a hot sunny day keeping the top layer of soil moist may take several times per day. It's not an exact science, if the soil is sticky and feels moist, it's moist enough. If you do not have irrigation, a few sprinklers on timers can save you quite a lot of time and assure you stay on schedule. You can find a few cheap hose timers and sprinklers or amazon or go to definitiveguidetoorganiclawncare.com to find my top picks for these products.

Water restrictions in your neighborhood?
Most towns allow new landscapes to be watered daily during their establishment, which is usually defined as a thirty day period. If not? Be stealthy, new seeds can't survive if they get wet then dry. There is tons of documentation on this and advisers in your town should know this and quite frankly it is unreasonable if they do not.

Watering practices can be the single element that makes the difference between a weak and a healthy lawn. It is important to cut back on watering as soon as your seedlings start popping above the straw layer. This can be either once a day or less depending on weather and what you are feeling with your finger. This time should be very early in the morning preferably one hour before sunrise. Avoid watering during the day unless grass seedlings start to show signs of stress. When watering during the day a percentage of your applied water evaporates, whereas watering during the early morning hours assures proper soil absorption. Additionally watering early at night is also not a suggested practice. This will leave your grass wet during the night and become more prone to diseases and algae.

During this period the grass is still quite sensitive to watering habits. Check the soil moisture levels at the heat of the day but this time check moisture levels at one inch below the surface. For more information on watering please see the watering chapter.

Protect your turf!

I'm not trying to make you the neighbor everyone hates but dogs and kids can wreak havoc on your newly seeded lawn. Dogs love digging in the mud, and kids love playing in it. With the amount of watering you are doing, that's probably what you've got. If you have a dog in the house make sure he or she is not digging up your new turf.

Simple footprints in your lawn while it is wet and soft can last years if not fixed right away so be sure to put a sign up. However, that may not be enough for kids or dogs that may be wondering in your neighborhood. If the lawn is small, you can surround the whole area with some roll-out plastic fencing available at hardware stores.

After germination

As your new lawn becomes established, start easing up on the water, depending on the weather. If you continue your everyday watering routine, you're likely to overdo it and cause disease and algae. Also, soil that is kept too wet will prohibit the growth of a deep root system.

When you have a pretty even ground cover of new seedlings, try skipping a day of watering. Watch the grass carefully on the second day. If the color starts to go from bright green to dull gray green or a purplish color, the grass needs water quickly. You may have to water some of these areas with a hose for quick recovery.

If the grass doesn't dry out, keep watering on an every other night schedule. This also depends heavily on weather. Hot windy days may require an extra watering cycle. While cloudy cool days might get you to stretch the watering till the third day. In arid climates you may find that watering every night is needed as well. For greater detail on watering please see the watering chapter.

Your first mowing

Wait for your new lawn to grow to 3 to 4 inches above the soil. Be sure to check and make sure your soil moisture is not too wet to avoid causing ruts and tearing up grass with your mower tires. Be sure to take great caution while turning if you are using a riding lawn mower. The root system has not matured enough yet for the twisting motion that's caused when tires turn on grass.

Your mower will most likely end up mulching lots of straw, so don't worry, this is actually beneficial. Over the weeks the mulching effect will add a source of organic matter for your new lawn. Don't mow with a mulching basket or bag, you want to keep what you have on the turf. For more information on mowing please refer to the mowing chapter.

Post germination fertilizing

The starter fertilizer you have already put down should have a lasting effect of about 3 months depending on how warm the weather has been and how active your soil microbes are. The application of your first post germination fertilizer should heavily overlap your starter. I suggest applying it 6 weeks after germination. This will kick your lawn into overdrive for the summer months.

Where your starter fertilizer was high in phosphorus your post germination fertilizer should be a higher percent in nitrogen. You should be looking for a 2-1-1 ratio or a 2-1-2 ratio applied at the rate of 1/2lb nitrogen per thousand. We will get into great detail over fertilizer ratios and calibration later within the fertilizer chapter.

Consider a 2nd Topdressing for warm season species

As touched upon earlier topdressing is the practice of covering your grass with a material to aide in its growth. For lawn care purposes the best material is sand. We use sand because we want our turf to be able to drain well. A well-drained soil provides stronger rooting, has a larger pore space for air circulation and creates a firmer surface. Sand topdressing is especially important for a warm season species as it dilutes the thatch layer (a layer of dead dying and decayed material) that warm season grasses naturally build very quickly.

A good sand topdressing should be done at around 4-6 weeks after seeding on warm season grass. This topdressing can greatly improve the grow-in process, help keep your lawn smooth and help dilute any thatch buildup.

The second topdressing should be considered a bonus step if you have topdressed your seed already. The amount of sand we are looking to apply here is ¼-½" thick. This heavy rate will cover a lot of grass blades but it will actually be highly beneficial. Apply sand first roughly with shovels, let dry and then spread with push brooms for best results.

Sodding

Though more expensive than seeding the installation of sod is a quick way to establish a new lawn. Most of the sod purchased is a blend of Kentucky bluegrass varieties or a mixture of other common turf grass types such as fine fescue, perennial ryegrass and tall fescue. One downside to laying sod instead of seed or sprigs is the additional thick mat layer you are introducing to your soil. This layer is caused from the aggressive fertilization practices at the sod farm needed to produce the most amount of product for its customers. This layer makes it difficult to grow a healthy root system and slows the water movement through your soil. In order to combat this an extra aerification should be performed the following growing season.

With proper irrigation, sod can be installed almost anytime during the growing season when the ground is not frozen or during the species natural dormancy period. The best time to plant sod however is early spring or fall. This gives the grass plenty of time to establish itself before the hot summer months or cold months of winter. As with seeding, these times of the year are usually very conducive to the environmental conditions needed for rapid establishment. It is best to avoid installing sod during very hot and dry conditions. Avoiding the hottest parts of the year will help in suppressing unwanted diseases.

Preparation

The same care and preparation for a seeded lawn should be implemented when doing a sodding project. With sod being an instant gratification grass usually inadequate consideration is often given to the sunlight requirements of each turf species. It is important to choose the right grass for the right situation whether it's from seed or sod.

To recap preparation:
1. Soil tests – Take soil samples and send away for testing (see soil test section)
2. Kill weeds – vinegar with a tsp. of dish soap in a small sprayer will work.
3. Till the soil – You can rent this machine and till to 4"
4. Add amendments – Suggested amendments from your soil testing results
5. Smooth the surface – Use a steel rake to flatten the surface.
For more details see seeding preparation.

Application

For both cool season and warm season grasses the application of sod remains the same. Speed is key. Plan ahead, when you receive your sod, you need to install immediately. The longer you leave the sod on the pallet the worse the end product will be. Employ the help of a few neighborhood kids or your family to get the job done quickly. Teaching them a few simple techniques while laying can make your project go smoothly.

The soil should be smooth and slightly moist. If needed, water the soil ahead of time very lightly. This improves the ability of the sod to survive and knit in faster. Lay the sod strips on the prepared soil tightly together, edge to edge, while staggering the seam ends so no two seams line up. Immediately soak the newly laid sod thoroughly enough to wet the soil beneath the installed sod.

As soon as it is dry enough to walk on, lightly roll the sod with the same type of roller we suggested within the seeding section. This will give good sod to soil contact and assure proper rooting.

Watering

Correct watering after installing the sod is critical to its survival. The idea is to keep the soil under the sod moist as well as the soil that comes with each sod piece. This does not mean constantly wet and soggy. Check on the moisture conditions from time to time by lifting the corners of the sod pieces. If the sod/soil seems excessively wet by the second day then delay watering until the third day. Water only when needed, keeping the soil moist but not overly wet. It is most important that you do not over-water and avoid saturating the sod/soil since this will prevent the sod from rooting and cause disease.

After the sod has rooted to the soil (from 1-2 weeks) it is important to change the watering schedule. Watering should be done thoroughly to soak the root zone but infrequently. Once the roots have knit into the soil (you can check by gently pulling upwards on the sod) then you shouldn't have to keep checking moisture levels with your fingers. Visual cues normally will suffice and you can begin watering normally during the early morning hours. To get detailed explanations on watering from here please see the watering chapter.

Don't be lead astray by neighbors, infrequent and deep watering creates a healthy root zone and discourages the onset of turf diseases. The idea is to push your grass to the point of almost getting dry spots as this will make the grass push roots downward. I can't count how many times I drive my golf cart past homes that are watering every single night rain or shine.

Mowing

Normally a newly installed sod lawn will require mowing as soon as the roots have knit into the soil. The height you choose to cut at should be dictated by the species you have chosen. That being said if the sod arrives very shortly mown then you may need to forego mowing until the target height has been met.

A couple of quick pointers here are to never remove more than 1/3 of the leaf blade in a single cut and do not use baskets or remove clippings from your new lawn. Mulching the clippings back into the root zone will help add valuable organic matter to the soil. For more information on mowing please visit our mowing section.

Fertilizing

I like applying a fertilizer a few weeks after sod has been laid or just after the sod has knitted into the soil. This assures the sod has all the nutrients necessary to develop a healthy root system from the start. Similar to the first fertilization of a seeded lawn you want a 1-2-1 ratio fertilizer with emphasis on phosphorus for a healthy root system. You can apply this fertilizer at the rate of 1lb of phosphorus per 1000sq feet. As always the nitrogen source should be a slow release organic form. We will get really detailed soon within the fertilization chapter on what this all means.

Remember the sod you purchased already has many nutrients within the root zone due to sod farms over fertilizing for production purposes. For this reason you really should be able to stretch your 2nd fertilizer application to 3 months after the first application. It is not as critical to fertilize within an 8 week period like seeding. The second fertilization can also have a higher nitrogen content with a ratio of 2-1-1 and the rate of 1/2lb of nitrogen per 1000sq feet.

Keep in mind these ratios are nearly impossible to achieve unless you are able to buy professional grade products. As this guide is read by both landscape business owners and homeowners alike I need to educate you on both sides of the spectrum. If you are a homeowner than Natural products such as Dr. Earth or Scotts Natural are available on amazon and will do a fine job, but it's only fair to educate you on the ideal ratios. I will get into greater detail about this within the fertilization chapter.

Sprigging

Sprigging a lawn is for warm season grasses only. The process of sprigging is simply spreading small individual grass plants instead of spreading seed. The preparation is almost the same as seeding but instead of top dressing immediately with sand or straw you will be burring the sprigs in the ground.

Late spring to early summer is the best time to plant. Tell your chosen turf nursery how many square feet of lawn you have, and the nursery will order the correct number of trays of plugs or bushels of sprigs. When your sprigs arrive, plant them as soon as possible. I have had sprigs arrive extremely dry. Dry enough to the point where I thought they were dead. I was able to bring them back with the help of a quick watering before planting. I doubt it will happen to you as I was in a 3rd world country but If it does happen to you I suggest misting the sprigs down as a first priority before planting. So please have a hose and nozzle ready prior to the sprigs getting there! The grass (if alive) will be able to take in the moisture it needs and the water will cool the overall temperature of the sprig down. Half of my career is just preventing catastrophes, and I hope at this point I've learned to prevent most of them.

Prep and plant
The same care and preparation for a seeded lawn should be implemented when doing a sprigging project with a few additions.

1. **Soil tests** – Take soil samples and send away for testing (see soil test section)
2. **Kill weeds** – vinegar with a tsp. of dish soap in a small sprayer will work.
3. **Till the soil** – You can rent this machine and till to 4"
4. **Add amendments** – Suggested amendments from your soil testing results

The next steps in the sprigging process can be done one of two ways, the standard method and my method. My method works best because it's fast if you have the right equipment, but the standard method works best for a homeowner of limited tools. First we will talk about the standard method.

Standard method: First you will make a grid for plantings. The object is to make rows 6" apart using the v-edge of a hoe at about 1-2" deep. The 6" spacing can be stretched to 8-10" to decrease costs but this will also increase the time needed to grow in your lawn. These v shaped rows will be where the sprigs are placed. Sprigs planted at 6" apart will cover your lawn twice as fast as rows planted at 6" apart. It's important to talk to your nursery on your plan on sprigging as they can adjust for the amount of sprigs needed.

Within each row sprigs should be placed 6" apart, keep your supplier in the know about your plan as these are just guidelines. It's important to keep your rows of accurate measurement as well, if you order sprigs based on 6" rows but instead placed 4" apart you will run out of sprigs before finishing the job.

Of course these are just general guidelines and instructions on your order may differ a bit from your planting pattern and it may be a good idea to talk to your supplier on what they suggest and to make sure you don't make haste in your planting pattern. The most important part is to make sure these rows are complete before your order arrives. Sprigs much like sod need to be planted as soon as they arrive at your doorstep.

When setting your plugs into your rows make sure root side is not facing upwards. Lay the sprigs in each row and then bury the bottom two thirds of the plants or so that some of the green of each sprig is above the soil surface. Once your planting is complete you may rake the planted area carefully to smooth the soil making sure not to disturb your sprigs. The next step is to roll the planted area with a lawn roller like the type we suggested in the seeded lawn establishment. If you cannot get your hands on a roller then using your mower's tires will suffice. Roll over the sprigs with either a roller or tires on the planted furrows to give the sprigs good soil contact.

Quick and dirty method: Much quicker if you have the proper tools. Step one is to call your supplier and give them the square footage of the area needing to be sprigged. Tell them you want to go heavy with the sprigging. They will do the math and send you the amount needed accordingly.

Next is to make sure your area is raked smooth, debris free and prepped for incoming sprigs. Once sprigs arrive you are going to spread smaller equal piles of sprigs evenly throughout your lawn. Once the piles have evenly placed you are going to rake the sprigs out smooth and even throughout your whole lawn.

Once the sprigs have been evenly spread give the whole area a good mist down to give the sprigs some moisture and then begin topdressing the whole area with ½" of sand. One 14 cubic yard dump truck full of sand will cover 10,000sqft with ½" of sand and will cost you about $700. The sand will take a few extra people to help with shovels and a broom at the end to get everything smooth. Once the finish broom has been completed you can water the entire area to the point of saturation. Be sure not to let any sand wash away.

The only downside to my method is that you have to have topdressing sand ready to go before the sprigs have arrived. With the standard method you don't need initial topdressing at all. I just find it very tedious and time consuming work planting each sprig in its row.

Watering
Watering is much of the same as the seeding process with a few differences. With the first watering after you have rolled in your sprigs is to make sure to wet the soil to the point of saturation. This amount of time can vary depending on your soil type and if you're using a simple hose or irrigation. With whatever method you are watering be sure to water gently to assure sprigs do not move around or runoff does not occur. I like to water to the point of almost puddling at first. In my experience sprigs end up growing in the fastest this way. After that you can get away with light watering or just enough to keep the top 1" of the soil moist.

It is a good idea to check soil moisture with your finger to gauge how many times a day you should be watering. For the first few days check every couple of hours as a barometer for the proper watering schedule. The same goes for how many minutes a day you can water. For example on a cloudy day you may be able to get away with one watering per day. It's not an exact science, if the soil is slightly sticky, it's moist enough. Adversely on a hot sunny day keeping the top layer of soil moist may take several times per day. If you do not have irrigation, a few sprinklers on timers can save you quite a lot of time and assure you stay on schedule.

Water restrictions?
Lots of towns allow new landscapes to be watered daily during their establishment period, which is usually defined as a thirty day period. If not? Be stealthy, new sprigs can't survive if they get wet then dry. There is enough proper documentation to support your cause and every town in America should have exceptions to accommodate.

As soon as your sprigs start to grow and roots are knitting into the soil it's time to cut back on watering. The timing should be very early in the morning preferably one hour before sunrise. The frequency of watering should be once per day. Again check soil moisture levels at the heat of the day and scout for signs of stress. A good indicator is wilting leaves that have lost their luster and have begun to shrivel. For more information on watering please see our watering section.

Fertilization
We are going to be using the same guidelines here as with the seeding process. Use a fertilizer high in phosphorus and potassium. This fertilizer should also have a slow release organic form of nitrogen. An inexpensive choice is Scotts Natural Lawn Food but its phosphorus and potassium content are quite frankly a little lower

than I like for a sprig grow-in. A more complete option would be Dr. Earth 715 Super Natural Lawn Fertilizer. It comes with higher phosphorus and potassium then the Scotts fertilizer. For best results plan on aiming for an application of 1/2lb of nitrogen. See fertilizer section for more details on calibrations and ratios needed.

Mowing

Before the first mowing do a walk-through of your new lawn and pull any weeds before you mow over them. Your first mow should happen when the soil is dry enough not to cause ruts from a mower and wait till the height of your grass is about 1-1.5" tall. Avoid tight turns if you have a riding lawn mower, you do not want to cause track marks or rip your newly planted grass. The amount of mowing is in relationship to the speed at which your new sprigs will spread. The more mowing performed means a quicker grow in. That being said, once you start mowing plan on doing so every 3 days for the first two weeks. After two weeks, you may continue with a once a week mowing frequency.

Topdressing (standard method)

If you do elect to use the standard method for sprigging you will still have to plan for a sand topdressing. This will aide in the grow-in process and usually needs to be done between 3-4 weeks post-planting. ½" of sand should suffice and be sure to smooth the sand as best as possible.

If you have chosen to use my method then a sand topdressing at this point is not needed. If extra sand is left over from the original process you may use it to topdress any weak areas you may have within the lawn.

6th week fertilizer app,

Much like with seeding the starter fertilizer you have already put down should have a lasting effect of about 3 months depending on how warm the weather has been and how active your soil microbes are. The application of your 6th week fertilizer app should heavily overlap your starter. This application should be made one month after your sprigs have started to spread which is usually about 6 weeks. This in effect will give your new lawn a one two punch and kick it into overdrive for the summer months.

Where your starter fertilizer was high in phosphorus your post germination fertilizer should be high in nitrogen. Choose a slow release nitrogen source such as Scotts Natural Lawn Food. As an inexpensive homeowner choice it's actually a pretty good organic fertilizer and readily available through amazon. Its high nitrogen content is perfect for quick top growth. The rate of this should be applied at 1/2lb of nitrogen per 1000sqft. For more information on fertilizers, soil sampling, rates and calibrations please see the fertilization chapter.

Over seeding

Over seeding is not what I would consider an organic practice. During the winter months when you want your overseeded lawn to shine the soil microbes are at their least active. For this reasoning in order to develop a lush over seeded lawn synthetic fertilizers (either IBDU or Nitrate) often have to be deployed in order to achieve your desired results. For the basis of a complete education I invite you to continue to read and judge accordingly.

Overseeing only pertains to lawns planted with warm season grasses within the transition zone. The transition zone is a region where both warm season grasses and cool season grasses can be grown. The warm season grasses will thrive in the summer but go dormant in the winter. While the cool season grasses can stay green all winter long but will die off in the summer. In this transition zone you can over seed your warm season grasses with a cool season variety for the winter months to keep a green lawn during a season where normally you're looking at dormant brown grass.

The over seeding process should happen a few months before the first frost of winter. As a general rule of thumb the last weeks in October or first weeks in November work well for the northern hemisphere. There are many ways to over seed. All of which I find far too time consuming and in my opinion not worth the trouble. Below are the steps needed to begin your overseed.

1. Prep your existing lawn by scalping it down to 3/4" – 1". Normally I would say never to bag your clippings but this is the exception to that rule. By bagging your mulched grass

you will assure your seeds to have good soil contact rather than sitting atop freshly cut grass clippings.

2. Verti-cut your lawn to remove thatch. Preferably in two directions. You can either have a company come and do this or you can use a dethatching rake. Rake up all your verticut debris or mow your lawn with the bagging unit attached. More on verti-cutting can be found within the cultivation chapter.

3. Don't over seed with annual ryegrass. Your best bet is to choose a winter tolerant perennial ryegrass variety. Scotts or Pennington sell good options for Perennial Ryegrass that requires less water than standard seed and get good results overall. You can look for entophyte enhanced ryegrass varieties but for over seeding purposes it's really a non-needed expense.

4. Much like seeding for a new lawn, calibrate your spreader to the rate suggested on the bag. This application rate can be anywhere from 2-4lbs per 1000sqft. I tend to lean on the heavy side of things for a quicker grow-in. I than usually take my chosen rate and cut it in half and spread in two different directions (two directions at half rate means a completed full rate) to assure even coverage, avoid skips and hide overlap. For more information on this see the section on calibration and application within the fertilization chapter. For people who have opted to use rotary spreaders remember that seeds will inevitably make it into undesired areas.

5. After you have spread your seed at the desirable rate make sure to fertilize your lawn with a slow release complete fertilizer focusing on nitrogen with a 2 parts nitrogen -1 part phosphorus – 2 parts potassium or even a 1-1-1 ratio (more on ratios later). Potassium during these fall and winter months will prove to be the most valuable nutrient for plant defense against snow molds and other cool temperature fungi.

6. Watering your over seeded lawn should be done a couple of times per day to make sure the top layer of soil remains moist until germination. Once your seedlings have popped you can than back the watering off to avoid over watering. Remember deep and infrequent watering of 2-3 times per week is the overall goal for any turf situation.

7. After 7-14 days your seed should germinate and you can mow about 1-2 weeks after that. This will give the grass plenty of time to root in before you mow. Remember to remove the bagging unit from your mower.

8. Your second fertilization has flexibility. You may apply as early as two months after your first application or you can wait till early spring. The microbes needed for organic conversions are not active during these cold months. There is no real hurry here, as the soil temperatures drop so does the activity of soil microbes. These microbes are needed to convert organic forms of nitrogen. It's not a massive concern because when the soil microbes slow so does the growth of your grass. I don't see it becoming a problem but if you do

see your grass loosing color in the late fall you may apply an IBDU (isobutylidene diurea) based slow release nitrogen source. It's not something I personally use but many golf course superintendents do. The reason being is that normal slow release nitrogen sources will not work well in the winter time. This includes organic forms and all other slow release synthetic sources as well. When temperatures drop soil microbes will not be active enough for the optimal degradation rates of these slow release products. IBDU on the other hand does not need soil microbes to feed your grass which make it perfect for colder temperatures.

Now I will say that IBDU is not organic and is intended for professional use so finding it as a homeowner can become tricky. If you cannot find a supplier for it there is a few options you have. One is to contact local landscaping companies who deal with lawn care and ask if they have any on hand could sell it to you. Also you can contact professional distributors like a Site One store. Lots of fertilizers that come with IBDU also have the nitrate form of nitrogen which is also good for winter time. This is a quick release form but if you cannot find IBDU anywhere nitrate forms of nitrogen might be your best bet.

Nitrates are a quick release I would not suggest applying heavier than 1/2lb nitrogen per 1000sq feet per application. Nitrate is not considered an organic product but applying it at low application rates will minimize any leaching that may occur. Leaching not only is unfriendly to the environment but is a waste of fertilizer. Popular nitrate forms are potassium nitrate, magnesium nitrate and calcium nitrate. When applying quick forms of nitrogen it is best to water the fertilizer in immediately after application to avoid turf burn.

Lastly since nitrate is a quick release form of nitrogen it needs to be applied every 4-6 weeks as opposed to an IBDU form which can last up to 12. For more information on fertilizer programs and calibration please see the fertilization chapter of this guide.

FERTILIZATION

Fertilizer basics

All plants require the same 16 essential elements as nutrients. Lawns require the macronutrients nitrogen (N), phosphorus (P) and potassium (K) in the greatest quantities. Calcium (Ca), Magnesium (Mg) and Sulfur (S) are required less frequently and in smaller quantities. The micronutrients Iron (Fe), Manganese (Mn), Zinc (Zn), Copper (Cu), Chlorine (Cl), Molybdenum (Mo) and Boron (B) are required in smaller quantities.

Fertilizers are often described by three numbers, such as 16-8-10 or 21-0-0. These three numbers indicate the percent of Nitrogen (N), Phosphorus (P), and Potassium (K) respectively. For example, a 16-8-10 fertilizer would contain 16% nitrogen, 8% phosphorus, and 10% potassium. Fertilizers that contain all three nutrients (nitrogen, phosphorus, and potassium) are referred to as complete fertilizers.

If a fertilizer has the analysis is 16-4-8, the fertilizer ratio is 4-1-2; a 14-7-14 analysis would have a 2-1-2 ratio. Generally mature lawns generally require more nitrogen than phosphorus and potassium (for the most part); therefore, ratios of 4-1-2 or 2-1-1 are commonly recommended. Turf maintenance fertilizers vary in nitrogen content and may contain a portion of the nitrogen as water-insoluble nitrogen (W.I.N.) or slowly available nitrogen.

The source of nitrogen in fertilizers influences nitrogen availability and response. There are two categories of nitrogen sources: quick release and slow release. Quick release nitrogen sources are water-soluble and can be readily utilized by the plant are susceptible to leaching and are available to the plant for a short period of time.

Quick release sources include Urea, Ammonium sulfate, and various combinations of nitrate such as Calcium nitrate, Magnesium Nitrate and Potassium Nitrate. Quick release nitrogen should never be applied at a rate exceeding 1/2lb/1000sqft as leaching will occur. Many tests have concluded that turf response will not benefit when quick release fertilizers are applied higher than this rate. Quick release sources of Nitrogen can last from 4-6 weeks depending on rainfall amounts.

Slow release nitrogen sources release their nitrogen over extended periods of time and are applied less frequently and can be applied higher rates than the quick release nitrogen sources. Slow release nitrogen can slowly feed the plant for up to 3 months which means even when applied at high rates slow release nitrogen has a very little leaching potential. Popular slow release synthetic sources include urea formaldehyde (UF), UF based products (methylene urea), urea triazanone, sulfur coated urea (SCU), isobutylidene diurea (IBDU). Popular 100% organic sources include bone meal, fish meal, crab meal, crab shell, feather meal, blood meal, sunflower hull ash, animal manures and activated sewage sludge. Some fertilizer products contain a mix of synthetic and organic so pay close attention to labels before buying fertilizers.

Most synthetic fertilizers containing such products as UF, MU, SCU and IBDU rarely are 100% slow release. Most synthetic fertilizers normally contain a mix of quick release and slow release formulas. For education purposes I think it's important for you to be able to identify these synthetic quick release formulas. Below is an example of a label containing both slow and fast release fertilizer.

Example fertilizer label:

> Guaranteed Analysis
> Total Nitrogen 16%
> 6% Water Insoluble Nitrogen (WIN)
> Available Phosphoric Acid (P2O5) 4%
> Soluble Potash (K2O)..8%

Now we can tell that the water insoluble amount is only about a third part of the total nitrogen here (6% / 16% = 37.5%). This means that most of the nitrogen is of a quick release form. It's important from there to do some further investigation and read to find what the fertilizer is derived from. Normally this is written below the analysis percentages.

If Water Insoluble Nitrogen not listed on the fertilizer label, one should assume it is all water-soluble or quick release nitrogen, unless the fertilizer label indicates it contains sulfur-coated urea. Sulfur-coated urea (SCU) fertilizers do provide slowly available nitrogen, but the fertilizer label does not list it as WIN. If the fertilizer contains sulfur-coated urea, include that portion as water-insoluble nitrogen when determining the amount of nitrogen that is slowly available.

Sustainable practices

I know you are already sold on the organic approach, but I still find it important to tell you why it's the best approach so bear with me. There is much confusion over whether to use organic or synthetic fertilizers on lawns. It is 100% true that the type of fertilizer makes no difference to the grass. Grasses absorb nitrogen only as nitrate or ammonical-nitrogen and both organic and synthetic can provide these sources through microbial action in the soil. Soil microbes have no preference to the type of fertilizers they convert to NH_4+ (ammonical nitrogen) or NO_3- (nitrate nitrogen). As a direct feeding mechanism organics have no direct benefit over synthetic sources to feed your lawn.

Indirectly however there are key differences between organic and synthetic fertilizers. One of these major indirect advantages to using organic fertilizer is humus. Once organic fertilizers are broken down by soil microbes humus is formed, and humus helps with water retention, nutrient retention and provides salt buffering. Adversely inorganic fertilizers actually add salts to the soil which can build in the soil and hurt the health of the turf and slow the activity of soil microbes.

Another great advantage is activating the microbe population that converts organic food sources to the elements your grass needs to thrive. I touched base on this briefly in the preface of this book. The microbes that convert synthetic fertilizers are different than the ones that break down organics. The organic microbes will help you by feeding on parasitic nematodes, thatch and ward away diseases.

Organic fertilizers serve as both fertilizers and soil conditioners; they feed both soil and plants. This is one of the most important differences between a synthetic approach and an organic approach toward soil care and fertilizing. Soluble synthetic fertilizers contain mineral salts that plant roots can absorb quickly. These salts do not provide a food source for soil microorganisms and earthworms, and will even repel earthworms because they acidify the soil. Over time, soils treated only with synthetic chemical fertilizers lose organic matter and the living organisms that help to build a quality soil. As soil structure declines and water-holding capacity diminishes, more and more of the chemical fertilizer applied will leach through the soil. In turn, it will take ever-increasing amounts of fertilizer to stimulate plant growth. This diminishing return will be compounded with the added salts building in the soil. However when you use organic fertilizers, you avoid subjecting your soil into this kind of condition.

Lastly, the one major benefit I see especially in south Florida is that organic fertilizers have no leaching potential. Most golf course superintendents here in south Florida are constantly watching the weather in hopes that their synthetic fertilizer applications are not washed through the rhizosphere (root zone) due to a heavy rain. For example I have applied 1/2lbN/1000sqft of crab shell and received seven inches of rain the week after. All of the crab shell released normally and fed the plant as intended. The reason is that organics are a material just like sand or dirt. You can't wash it through the soil. This material is slowly broken down and as it's broken down it is immediately taken up by grass roots.

Synthetic fertilizers cannot be labeled as a sustainable practice. The conversion over to organic products has started happening within the golf course industry. The superintendent that haven't already started are far behind. There are far too many benefits to organics with no negative effects. The synthetic companies are still trying to hold on tight but it's an inevitable change coming in our industry. The ones holding onto synthetics are either set in their ways or ignorant to the science. Adding salts to soil, hurting micro and macro biology and leaching all add up to too many problems for any turf situation. With leaching potential being the greatest concern, quick release synthetics pose an environmental threat if applied incorrectly. If application has been completed before a large rain or irrigation has been applied too heavily the product can pass the rhizosphere and unable to be utilized by the plant. In time this nitrogen will be leached into the water table and cause a host of problems for the environment.

How to start your program
Fertilizer programs should be based off from your soil test results. This is the best way to ensure you are maintaining a sustainable lawn and being a steward to the environment. However that being said I am a big advocate of the lean and mean strategy to turf care. Establishment is one thing, I realize you need to use a bit more fertilizer than normal to make your grass grow in as fast as possible, but when you are simply maintaining your turf grass, less is more. Plants growing at limited nutrient supply invest more resources in the elaboration of the root system than over fertilized plants.

This lean and mean strategy is rarely used by any lawn care services. Generally speaking large fertilizer application companies follow the same fertilizer scheduling for all of their customers. They do not follow soil testing results to mix up special fertilizers or different schedules for every lawn they manage. If you are thinking of hiring a company to perform fertilizer applications to your lawn consider asking them a few questions. If they refuse to answer these questions walk away and find another company.

1. Will you be performing soil tests on my lawn prior to implementing a fertilizer program?
2. At what rates of nitrogen per year are you planning on using?
3. Are the products you are using slow release formulas or organic formulas?
4. How often will you be applying fertilizers to my lawn?

The answers you are looking for are as follows:

1. "Yes we preform soil tests on all of our customer's lawns before we make a fertilizer plan that's developed custom to fit your soil's needs." The only other acceptable answer is if they were to do tissue analysis. But for home lawn situations I don't even recommend this. It has to be performed monthly and doubtful that any company could give you that level of commitment. So if they don't do soil tests, look elsewhere.

2. "We are planning on trying about 2lbs of Nitrogen per 1000sqft the first year and then work off from feedback from you as a home owner to try and get that down to a lower number for the following years." 2lbs is a general number for most grasses per year, for Bermuda it's more like 4-6lbs depending on climate. More importantly you are looking for them to want to lower that number slowly based off from feedback from you as a customer. The feedback being "how often do you have to cut your grass?" "Does your grass

remain green year long?" "Does your grass growth seem to slow down its growth between fertilizer applications?" The reason being is that too much nitrogen is not a good thing, like I said earlier, too much fertilizer can be detrimental to your roots and cause other disease and thatch issues as well.

3. "We apply a mix of slow and quick release so your grass will be evenly fed throughout the year." Or "We apply a fully organic solution to your grass which gives your grass the optimal nutrition it needs year round." Both are acceptable with the latter being the better answer. As we discussed earlier, organics always beat synthetic fertilizers. Anything quick release is not going to give you good results and is not environmentally friendly.

4. "We apply fertilizers once every few months to perfectly space applications so that your grass does not have any peaks and valleys in its available nutrition." Or "We try to space out our applications based off from the conditions of your grass and feedback from you." Another excepted solution is for them to complete monthly applications at lower rates. It's considered a best practice to spoon feed any nutrient at very low rates. But usually companies do not do this as it takes too long to fertilize all of their clients each month. Avoid any answers like "We usually just go by how your lawn looks." That's a clear sign of ignorance on fertilization all together.

Some fertilizer companies will come out and look at your lawn and base a fertilizer program from what they see rather then what definitive evidence from a lab would tell them. Despite what anybody tells you, looking at a plant does not tell you the exact needs of the soil. They may be able to get close and guess that your lawn is lacking nitrogen or its deficient in some other nutrient but they will not be able to tell you by exactly how much. This is one reason you can fertilize your own lawn more effectively by yourself rather than employing a company. Most customers of companies like these measure the health of a lawn by the hue of green it possess. It only pays for these companies to overfeed a lawn in order to keep the top growth of the lawn green. A green lawn is a happy customer. The tactic does keep your lawn green but it will also create optimal conditions for disease, insect infestations and limit the growth of your roots. This is by design as you will have to pay for added visits by your fertilizer company to alieve the problems. Your goal is to build a sustainable lawn that will save money on water and limit disease and insect outbreaks. Keeping a limited but constant nutrient supply is always best.

Landscaping companies cannot create lawn care that is custom fabricated to your turf grass and soil's unique needs. This is just not economical for them. They rely on homeowners to stay ignorant to the fact that their whole system for homeowner lawn care is inherently flawed. For example, when I maintain a golf course I treat each hole on the course differently and I use my soil test results from each hole as my guide for fertilization. Even though golf courses are only spread out across several hundred acres that is more than large enough to create soil inconsistencies. When you consider that a company maintaining lawns may be providing services spread out across 50 miles or more the nutrient needs differ drastically. One mix for all clients in their service area is not the correct way to care for your lawn. In this respect it becomes laughable for any company providing these types of services to be called an environmentally friendly practice.

The following portion of this chapter will cover an example scenario of a soil test and how to go about creating a fertilizer plan and schedule to maintain a healthy lawn. Again no two soil situations are the same, the example only demonstrates how you would split up your applications. First you will see the actual soil report from one of my last golf courses I was in charge of growing in. Second you will see the soil recommendations done by the agronomist that works at the lab. Lastly I will walk you through a plan of action based from the recommendations pretending that the soil report is for your lawn.

Soil testing

Soil testing is an essential step before starting your fertilizer program. In this process the 16 elements needed for plant growth are removed from the soil and measured to see the quantities of these elements are available to your plants. After the quantities are assessed they then can make fertilizer recommendations for you depending on your turf species.

Aside from measuring plant available nutrients soil testing also measures your soil pH, organic matter and exchangeable acidity. These measurements are needed to quantify the amounts of amendments you may need to add to your soil. These can include lime to raise pH, sulfur to lower pH or gypsum to flush excess salts and/or correct calcium and magnesium imbalances.

When your soil testing has concluded, either my laboratory or the lab you have chosen will send you detailed information on amendment and fertilizer recommendations. These amendments can then be applied along with the creation of a fertilizer program based from your soil tests. By following your soil test report you will take out the need for guess work and ultimately save money on your fertilizer inputs.

By following soil reports you will also promote a sustainable and environmentally friendly lawn. Applying accurate quantities of fertilizer needed for your unique situation reduces nutrient runoff into surface or ground water.

If you already are maintaining your current lawn the best time to take soil samples is just before your next fertilizer application. Soil samples taken after fertilization will be inaccurate because nutrients from your fertilizer application have yet to be taken up by your plants and still reside in the soil. If you are about to grow in a new lawn be sure to take soil samples 1-2 months before grassing. This will give you ample time to get your soil reports back and the purchase the necessary amendments and fertilizers before your project starts.

Most universities horticulture or agriculture department do soil testing at very little cost to you. This is a great inexpensive solution and will suffice for most homeowner's needs.

How to take soil samples:

1. Request soil sample bags from your local soil testing laboratory. You may also use plastic Ziploc bags if you wish. The lab will then transfer into their bag once you bring in your sample. One pint of soil should suffice for soil testing needs.

2. Collect your needed tools – Small bucket and soil probe or small shovel. Do not to use copper tools as this will skew the results of your testing.

3. Dig to a depth of 4" and then gather a handful or two from the bottom of the hole to place in your bucket. Soil collected at a 4" depth is generally considered to return the most accurate reading.

4. Repeat this process from 8-10 locations spread throughout your lawn. Be sure to pick out any rocks or grass/weeds from your bucket you may have collected in your sample. Roots within the sample are fine to keep.

5. When you have finished collecting your samples mix the soil together in the bucket and then collect 16-24oz of soil into a Ziploc type plastic bag or a soil sample bag which can be purchased on amazon.

6. Ship or bring in your soil samples to the laboratory. If given the option get the full lineup of testing done on you soil. It's a bit more expensive but they will check every single element for you. If you would like my lab to do the testing for you more information can be found at definitiveguidetoorganiclawncare.com

When receiving your soil reports there are a few important things to note here. Laboratories usually fill these reports with graphs and numbers which are hard to understand unless you have a firm understanding of soil science. I generally tell my clients to only look at the recommendation section and only briefly skim over the results section. If you need me to decipher any vague reports or need my lab to complete soil testing along with a comprehensive recommendation go to definitiveguidetoorganiclawncare.com for more information.

Soil reports

The reports on the next few pages were from my golf course in the Caribbean on the island of Curacao. The soil there is extremely high in salts and extremely low on macronutrients such as phosphorus. The soil conditions on the island were actually toxic to most plants due to its extremely high salt content. The pH was also extremely high and difficult to manage but with the help of my soil report and recommendations I was able to come up with a fertilizer plan that best controlled the conditions of the soil.

NOTE: As a home owner you will not find soil conditions like this. There are not too many places in the world with soil like this but it will be good to show you how exactly we can alleviate even the worst of conditions with a proper soil report.

Soil taken from #6 Fairway

Sample Information			
Sample	6 FAIRWAY	Sampled	10-08-2012
Lab Number	B20424	Tested	10-30-2012

Analysis		Result	Optimal	Analysis		Result	Optimal
Soil pH		7.8	6.5-7.5	Sulfur	m3-ppm	97	20-40
Buffer pH				Boron	m3-ppm	3.4	1.7-2.6
Organic Matter	%	3.6		Copper	m3-ppm	5.3	Varies
CEC		33.4		Iron	m3-ppm	150	9-40
K Saturation	%	2.5	2.0-4.0	Manganese	m3-ppm	140	Varies
Mg Saturation	%	36.1	10-20	Zinc	m3-ppm	2.6	3.9-10.9
Ca Saturation	%	45.0	50-70	Sodium	m3-ppm	1259	
Na Saturation	%	16.4	0-10	Soluble Salts	mmhos/cm	0.77	0.00-4.00
K/Mg Ratio		0.2		Nitrate-N	ppm	9	
Ca/Mg Ratio		4.8					
Phosphorus	m3-ppm	23	30-60				
Potassium	m3-ppm	389	260-380				
Magnesium	m3-ppm	1642	330-550				
Calcium	m3-ppm	7817	4400-6300				

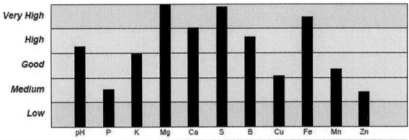

Recommendations		Nutrients expressed in broadcast lbs/1000 sqft, except Fe (foliar) and Mn (row)										
Yr	Crop	CaCO3	N	P2O5	K2O	Mg	S	B	Cu	Fe	Mn	Zn
13	Paspalum, Seashore, Turf	0	4.0	2.0	1.0	0.0	10.3	0.0	0.0	0.0	0.0	0.1

Soil taken from the Practice Tee

Sample Information			
Sample	PRACTICE	Sampled	10-08-2012
Lab Number	B20426	Tested	10-30-2012

Analysis		Result	Optimal	Analysis		Result	Optimal
Soil pH		7.9	6.5-7.5	Sulfur	m3-ppm	15	20-40
Buffer pH				Boron	m3-ppm	2.2	1.7-2.6
Organic Matter	%	4.7		Copper	m3-ppm	1.4	Varies
CEC		25.2		Iron	m3-ppm	73	9-40
K Saturation	%	2.6	2.0-4.0	Manganese	m3-ppm	51	Varies
Mg Saturation	%	27.6	10-20	Zinc	m3-ppm	1.9	3.9-10.9
Ca Saturation	%	59.6	50-70	Sodium	m3-ppm	588	
Na Saturation	%	10.2	0-10	Soluble Salts	mmhos/cm	0.19	0.00-4.00
K/Mg Ratio		0.3		Nitrate-N	ppm	6	
Ca/Mg Ratio		6.4					
Phosphorus	m3-ppm	5	30-60				
Potassium	m3-ppm	307	230-340				
Magnesium	m3-ppm	949	300-490				
Calcium	m3-ppm	6112	3400-4700				

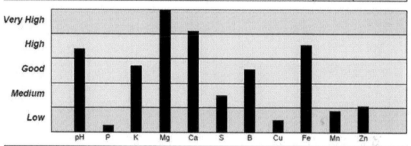

Recommendations		Nutrients expressed in broadcast lbs/1000 sqft, except Fe (foliar) and Mn (row)										
Yr	Crop	CaCO3	N	P205	K2O	Mg	S	B	Cu	Fe	Mn	Zn
13	Paspalum, Seashore, Turf	0	4.0	4.0	1.6	0.0	11.2	0.0	0.0	0.0	0.1	0.1

Soil test taken from #16 green.

Sample Information			
Sample	16 GREEN	Sampled	10-08-2012
Lab Number	B20429	Tested	10-30-2012

Analysis		Result	Optimal	Analysis		Result	Optimal
Soil pH		8.5	6.5-7.5	Sulfur	m3-ppm	137	20-40
Buffer pH				Boron	m3-ppm	3.0	1.7-2.6
Organic Matter	%	0.9		Copper	m3-ppm	0.5	Varies
CEC		27.4		Iron	m3-ppm	5	9-40
K Saturation	%	0.4	2.0-4.0	Manganese	m3-ppm	5	Varies
Mg Saturation	%	39.8	10-20	Zinc	m3-ppm	1.0	3.9-10.9
Ca Saturation	%	54.8	50-70	Sodium	m3-ppm	311	
Na Saturation	%	4.9	0-10	Soluble Salts	mmhos/cm	0.17	0.00-4.00
Ca/Mg Ratio		63.7		Nitrate-N	ppm	9	
Phosphorus	m3-ppm	1	30-60				
Potassium	m3-ppm	51	230-350				
Magnesium	m3-ppm	1485	310-500				
Calcium	m3-ppm	94599	3600-5100				

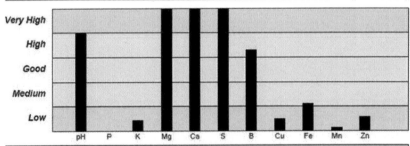

Recommendations			Nutrients expressed in broadcast lbs/1000 sqft, except Fe (foliar) and Mn (row)									
Yr	Crop		CaCO3	N	P2O5	K2O	Mg	S	B	Cu	Fe	Mn	Zn
13	Paspalum, Seashore, Turf		0	4.0	4.0	5.1	0.0	20.9	0.0	0.0	0.0	0.1	0.2

Lab given recommendations

"In general, there are 3 areas soil tested — Greens, Fairways and Practice Areas. There ae some general observations.

1. Phosphorus is in short supply for all areas. Phosphorus provides the energy within the plant. The lack of P reduces the overall health of the turf. This can be seen in roots,
color and wear tolerance. The P levels need to be improved.

2. Sodium Levels are off the chart. This is Paspalum which is salt tolerant. With sodium levels at 9+%, and calcium levels on the low Side, there needs to be an adjustment to the calcium levels.

3. Many of the nutrients are off the chart. This is an Indication that these nutrients are tied up m the soil. These nutrients can be stripped from the soil with an organic fertilizer due to the increase in microbial stripping these nutrients. Plus, the program needs to add these high level nutrients back to the soil.

4. Micronutrients are tied up due to the high pH level. These nutrients are essential to many
of the internal plant processes. Without adequate levels of these nutrients, the turf will be weak and prone to problems.

Soil Test General Solutions

In general, there are some minor program and product changes that can be made to overcome
many of the above concerns.

1. Phosphorus availability is managed in a couple of ways - use traditional P sources like MAP to build levels and use organic nutrient sources to strip and deliver die P. The first issue is to build than strip the P with organic fertilizer products. The general rule is 85% of P is delivered by soil microbes. This requires applications of an organic product.

2. Sodium levels can be managed several ways - leach sodium with wetting agents and the addition of calcium. This addresses both the high sodium levels and the low calcium
levels. Plus, the addition of the calcium helps to strip the other tied up nutrients.

3. Add an organic fertilizer to strip nutrients that are tied up in the soil. A biological product delivery system is not restricted by the pH, sodium levels or nutrients levels to deliver these nutrients. The limiting factor is oxygen. Aeration needs to be an added
aspect for this process.

4. Micronutrients can be applied in liquid form. The Sanctuary has a number of liquid polysaccharide micronutrients that are taken up by the tissue and the roots. These polysaccharide products deliver the nutrients and feed the soil system.

Nutrient Overviews

1. pH — *the soil pH is high at around 7.8+, which cannot be changed but, will dictate some nutrient limitations that need to be addressed with product choices. At pH level,*

traditional nutrients can be enhanced with the use of biological Imputes. This can improve traditional nutrients release. Or, a hybrid organic containing these nutrients can be as effective. Traditional nutrients can be applied effectively to build nutrient levels in

die soil. An organic fertilizer application can help to improve die delivery of these traditional nutrients. The key issue is that nutrient levels need to be adjusted to address

availability. In addition at these pH levels, micronutrients will be less available to the

plant. These micronutrients will be tied up in the soil. These micronutrients are very essential to plant health. Select biological micronutrients to improve their availability.

2. Nitrogen is essential for turf quality. Nitrogen is required for protein synthesis, which is critical to overall turf health. Nitrogen is essential for stress tolerance, disease & wear tolerance and overall turf quality. The soil report indicates that nitrogen levels are low for greens. The fairways have a good OM level that a biological fertilizer can help to release to the turf. The limiting factor is gas or oxygen levels. Water

management and mechanical renovation is essential.

3. Phosphorus — *Phosphorus is the energy nutrient that is required for photosynthesis within the turf. The phosphorus levels are subpar and much of the P is tied up in the system. A key principle is that most of P is made available by microbial release. In moving*

forward, the P levels need to be increased and an organic nutrient needs to be

added. I
would use a traditional product that blends MAP and calcium as part of a
nutrient building program. The Sanctuary 12-2-12 or IS-2-6 are good options.

4. Potassium — this nutrient level is marginal on the greens. Potassium will build wear and
stress tolerance. Potassium is essential for nutrient and water uptake. Plus, potassium is required to manage wear tolerance. Potassium needs to be increased each month to enhance the turf quality.

5. Calcium - is essential for stress tolerance. The Ca levels are substantially low. The Ca can be applied as both a granular product monthly or as a soluble product during peak periods of stress. Plus, the use acid would also help increase the amount available.

6. Micro nutrients — these are essential nutrients for many of the turf internal hormonal or enzyme requirements. Micro nutrients are critical for overall turf quality and health. The soil reports indicate an elevated level of these nutrients. But, the high pH level is limiting the availability. The Sanctuary polysaccharide products offer excellent options.

7. Organic Matter The OM provides 2 critical aspects to turf management — nitrogen reserves and microbial food energy. The soil tests show that there is very little nitrogen reserves on the greens but is ample on the fairway. The OM levels can be reduced by the addition of an organic product.

Program Recommendations

1. *Greens* —*The Sanctuary several products that would improve the overall quality of the turf and improve the health of the soil. Sanctuary 12-1-12 (40 SGN) can be applied at 3 bags/A monthly. After aeration, the applied rate is 5 bags/A. In addition, the Sanctuary has several bio liquid products. This would Include Micro Turf containing Fe, Zn, and Cu. This should be applied monthly at the 12oz/A rate. Plus, Vitality containing Calcium Nitrate and Chelated Calcium should be applied at the 12oz rate/month. Lastly, Sanctuary Poly K 0-0-24 should be applied at 16oz/A/month or on a 21 day interval during peak periods of stress. There are 2 other Sanctuary products to consider. These are Sanctuary Tea and Resilience. Tea is a bio liquid that contains amino acids, sugars, and potassium and calcium nitrate. This is an outstanding stress fighter nitrogen product. Next, Resilience, which contains some of the basic components as Tea but is a bio P and Ca source. In addition to the Sanctuary products, a high quality turf calcium be applied at 4 to 6lbs/1000/month this needs to be increased to 10 to 12lbs/1000/month at time of aeration. Lastly, a good infiltrating wetting agent should be used to manage water and sodium.*

2. *Fairways - The Sanctuary 12-2-12 + minor is an excellent product to address key nutrient deficiencies. This should be applied at S bag/A on S to 12 week interval pending color response and clipping yields. This product will help to release tied up nutrients in the soil. In addition, a traditional product that contains MAP and calcium plus a slow release nitrogen source be combined. This is a soil building application for P and Ca. I can recommend a specific blend to complement the Sanctuary product. To supplement color, Sanctuary Iron NE is a biological iron source that offer excellent color at 12 oz/A. This can be applied on a 3 week Interval. Or, the Sanctuary Micro Turf can also be used to provide a* *broader scope of micronutrients.*

In summary, the soil test shows that the nutrient levels can be managed with some minor changes to the program. Please review this information. I will be at the meeting in December San Juan. I would welcome the opportunity to meet with you and further discuss specific product and program recommendations."

Fertilizer plan

Based from this recommendation we can come up with an educated plan of action. To keep things from getting confusing let's make believe that this is your actual soil report on your lawn. Do not be intimidated by the amounts of products and application rates just yet. This is not a typical soil and no lawn you will maintain will have soil anywhere near this bad.

The main issue you want to understand is the "General Solutions" on the first page of the soil report. This is the agronomist or soil scientist's recommendations to alleviate soil problems. In our case the soil was very low in Phosphorus, high in salts, low in organic matter and had many tied up nutrients and it was suggested to add micronutrients. I will say that the soil recommendations from the lab aren't all that strong and I have long since stopped using this laboratory for my soil testing. However no matter who you choose as you're likely not to get mind blowing recommendations in line with our organic principles but its great practice to see how we can make really good recommendations based off the report.

At this point we know the benefits of organic fertilizers and the role they play with buffering salts and increasing soil health. Considering soil microbes the workers of the soil and as long as we are feeding them with the proper organic materials they will take care of many soil conditions we are facing in this soil example. Using organics in this situation will give us salt buffering, soil microbes to free tied up nutrients and provide essential nitrogen and phosphorus to the soil. Knowing this we can do some shopping on appropriate fertilizers for the year. It's going to be impossible to find one bag of fertilizer that fulfills every requirement needed. In this case you will have to apply several different fertilizers throughout the year to accomplish your goals. I have chosen the readily available organic fertilizers (mostly on amazon) below and shown how each can help us fulfill the recommendations.

Bone Meal (3-15-0): To boost calcium and phosphorus. This is a very slow release.

Cotton seed meal (4-3-6): Natural acidifier and will help us lower pH. The complete analysis will add needed potassium to the soil as well. Be sure to only buy 100% organic cotton seed meal. Some cotton seed meals are not organic and carry pesticides within them.

Dr. Earth gold (4-4-4): Complete analysis providing needed nitrogen, phosphorus and potassium.

Dr. Earth super (9-3-5): Complete analysis providing needed nitrogen, phosphorus and potassium. This will carry a different blend of micronutrients than the 4-4-4.

Earthworm castings: This will help build up organic material in the soil and add diverse soil microbes. A whole book can be written on the benefits of earthworm casting teas, extracts and straight castings. If we did not need the added organic materials I would suggest earthworm casting tea (if self-brewing) or extract (long shelf life).

Humic acid: Considered a bio-stimulant this organic material will help free up micronutrients from the soil and add a much needed organic source. Not all Humic acids are created equal. I have found

Humate International out of Jacksonville Florida sells a superior product.

Seaweed extract: Another bio-stimulant this will keep your grass healthy during stressful periods. Not all seaweeds are created equal. Be sure to only buy an extract that has been extracted only from *Ascophyllum nodosum.* This species has been shown in studies to be a superior stress reliever when applied to plants.

Gypsum (Calcium sulfate): Naturally mined Calcium sulfate is used for flushing salts and add needed calcium to the soil. Be sure you are not buying the dehydrate form of gypsum. Anhydrous is not as water soluble and worthless for flushing salts from soil.

Organic chelated micronutrients: This will help introduce micro nutrients in our soil. Be sure to look for OMRI organic certified products. I like Eco MicroBoost. It's got a good analysis of micronutrients and is 100% organic.

By adding up the 4 fertilizers we find that the average analysis is 4-5-3 which is actually really close to perfect for our needs in this example. In time this blend will help repair the soil and create a good growth media for our grass. Now we are going to implement these products into a fertilizer plan and I will talk you through the rates and timing of each. Again don't be intimidated, this plan is only based upon the soil test results above.

Cool season grass:

Application 1 (April or when ground is thawed)

3-15-0 @ 1/2N/1000sqft
Gypsum @ 15lbs/1000sqft
Organic Micronutrient @ 3oz/1000sqft

Application 2 (June or three months after first application)

4-3-6 @ 1/2lbN/1000sqft
Seaweed extract @ 3oz/1000sqft
Gypsum @ 15lbs/1000sqft (applied during aerification while holes are open)
Earthworm castings @ 10lbs/1000sqft (applied during aerification while holes are open)
Organic Micronutrient @ 3oz/1000sqft

Application 3 (August or three months after second application)

9-3-5 @ 1/2lbN/1000sqft + 0-4-34 @ 1/4lbK/1000sqft (sunflower hull ash)
Seaweed extract @ 3oz/1000sqft
Organic Micronutrient @ 3oz/1000sqft

Application 4 (October or two months after third application)

Granular humic acid @ 15lbs/1000sqft
Organic Micronutrient @ 3oz/1000sqft

Important – Regardless of your soil sample test results you will want to make at least four applications per season with the total amount of nitrogen adding up to 1.5lbsN/1000/year for a cool season grass variety. This will assure that your grass has a continuous feed of the proper amount of nitrogen and avoids peaks and valleys in nutrient availability. Keeping a constant slow feed of nitrogen is a best practice to warding off many problems such as diseases, insects and weeds.

The total amount of nitrogen per year however should always be subject to change. We are using 1.75lbs/year simply as a starting point. If you start to notice dollar spot on your lawn than you may want to raise your total amount of nitrogen per year by 1/4lb (2lbs of N per year total). I would achieve this by applying straight blood meal fertilizer that you can find on amazon during the months you notice a leaning of the color of turf. Avoiding this extra application during summer months should be considered the best practice. During these months you need to be careful about extra nitrogen applications as pythium and other root borne diseases can thrive. Also high nitrogen levels during fall months can prevent your grass from naturally hardening off for winter which is why I've suggested to only apply granular humic acid the example above.

To aid in the natural hardening off process cool season grasses go through during the fall months I have added a quarter pound application of sunflower hull ash in august. The slow burn potassium will stay within the soil going into winter. Potassium has shown to be highly beneficial for turf going into winter. We have chosen the month of august as microbes are still active due to high temperatures. An application of sunflower hull ash in October would be far too late for microbial breakdown.

Lastly, do not take soil samples immediately after a fertilizer application as this can skew test results. Its best practice to gather samples before or several weeks after a fertilizer application.

Warm season grass – Transitional zone:

Application 1 (Feb/March or when grass is coming out of dormancy)

> 3-15-0 @ 1/2N/1000sqft
> Seaweed extract @ 3oz/1000sqft
> Gypsum @ 15lbs/1000sqft
> Organic Micronutrient @ 3oz/1000sqft

Application 2 (May or three months after first application)

> 4-3-6 @ 1/2lbN/1000sqft
> Organic Micronutrient @ 3oz/1000sqft

Application 3 (July or two months after second application)

> 9-3-5 @ 1/2lbN/1000sqft
> Gypsum @ 15lbs/1000sqft (applied during aerification while holes are open)
> Earthworm castings @ 10lbs/1000sqft (applied during aerification while holes are open)
> Organic Micronutrient @ 3oz/1000sqft

Application 4 (October or two months after third application)

> 4-4-4 @ 1/2lbN/1000sqft
> Granular humic acid @ 15lbs/1000sqft
> Seaweed extract @ 3oz/1000sqft
> Organic Micronutrient @ 3oz/1000sqft

Important – Regardless of your soil sample test results you will want to make four applications per season with the total amount of nitrogen adding up to 2lbsN/year. If you are growing Bermudagrass within the transitional zone I would then suggest to use 3lbsN/year (use 4 split applications of 3/4lbN/1000 instead of 1/2lbN/1000).

This will assure that your grass does not have times with high amounts of nutrients available and times of low amounts of nutrients available (peaks and valleys). Keeping a constant feed of nutrients is a best practice to warding off many problems that can plague your lawn such as diseases.

The total amount of nitrogen per year however should always be subject to change. We are using 2lbs/year simple as a starting point. If your grass is not as green as you would like or you notice yellowing in between fertilizer applications than you may want to raise your total amount of nitrogen per year by 1/2lb (2.5lbs of N per year total). Adversely if you find your grass always green and have trouble keeping up with mowing due to grass that is growing too fast you may want to back off by 1/2lb per year (1.5lbs of N per year total). This number can take up to 4 years to get a perfect bead on what your lawn needs for nitrogen.

Again do not take soil samples immediately after a fertilizer application as this can skew test results.

Warm season grass – Tropical/Subtropical zone:
Application 1 (January)

> 3-15-0 @ 1/2N/1000sqft
> Seaweed extract @ 3oz/1000sqft
> Gypsum @ 15lbs/1000sqft
> Organic Micronutrient @ 3oz/1000sqft

Application 2 (March)

> 4-3-6 @ 1/2lbN/1000sqft
> Seaweed extract @ 3oz/1000sqft
> Organic Micronutrient @ 3oz/1000sqft

Application 3 (June)

> 9-3-5 @ 1/2lbN/1000sqft
> Granular humic acid @ 15lbs/1000sqft (applied during aerification while holes are open)
> Earthworm castings @ 10lbs/1000sqft (applied during aerification while holes are open)
> Gypsum @ 15lbs/1000sqft (applied during aerification while holes are open)
> Organic Micronutrient @ 3oz/1000sqft

Application 4 (August)

> 4-3-6 @ 1/2lbN/1000sqft
> Organic Micronutrient @ 3oz/1000sqft

Application 5 (October)

> 4-4-4 @ 1/2lbN/1000sqft
> Seaweed extract @ 3oz/1000sqft
> Organic Micronutrient @ 3oz/1000sqft

Important – Regardless of your soil sample test results you will want to make five applications per season with the total amount of nitrogen adding up to 2.5lbs/year. This amount of N is high for Paspalum and low for Bermudagrass. Please continue reading for a special application plan for each species.

The total amount of nitrogen per year however should always be subject to change. We are using 2.5lbs/year simple as a starting point. If your grass is not as green as you would like or you notice yellowing in between fertilizer applications than you may want to raise your total amount of nitrogen per year by 1/2lb (3lbs of N per year total). Adversely if you find your grass always green and have trouble keeping up with mowing due to grass that is growing too fast you may want to back off by 1/2lb per year (2lbs of N per year total). Another good indicator of too much nitrogen is your thatch layer. If you are having trouble maintaining a ½" layer of thatch back off your nitrogen amounts 1/2lb per year (2lbs of N per year total).

Paspalum species – Tropical/Subtropical zone:

Application 1 (January)

> 3-15-0 @ 1/2N/1000sqft + 0-4-34 @ 1/4lbK/1000sqft (sunflower hull ash)
> Seaweed extract @ 3oz/1000sqft
> Gypsum @ 15lbs/1000sqft
> Organic Micronutrient @ 3oz/1000sqft

Application 2 (March)

> 4-3-6 @ 1/3lbN/1000sqft + 0-4-34 @ 1/4lbK/1000sqft (sunflower hull ash)
> Seaweed extract @ 3oz/1000sqft
> Organic Micronutrient @ 3oz/1000sqft

Application 3 (June)

> 9-3-5 @ 1/2lbN/1000sqft
> Earthworm castings @ 10lbs/1000sqft (applied during aerification while holes are open)
> Granular humic acid @ 15lbs/1000sqft (applied during aerification while holes are open)
> Gypsum @ 15lbs/1000sqft (applied during aerification while holes are open)
> Organic Micronutrient @ 3oz/1000sqft

Application 4 (August)

> 4-3-6 @ 1/3lbN/1000sqft + 0-4-34 @ 1/4lb/1000sqft (sunflower hull ash)
> Organic Micronutrient @ 3oz/1000sqft

Application 5 (October)

> 4-4-4 @ 1/3lbN/1000sqft

Seaweed extract @ 3oz/1000sqft
Organic Micronutrient @ 3oz/1000sqf

Potassium is the first line of defense against diseases in Paspalum. The added slow release potassium in sunflower hull ash will keep an even amount available within the soil.

Bermudagrass – Tropical/Subtropical zone:

Application 1 (January)

> 3-15-0 @ 1/2N/1000sqft + 13-0-0 @ 1/2lbN/1000sqft (blood meal)
> Organic Micronutrient @ 3oz/1000sqft
> Gypsum @ 15lbs/1000sqft
> Seaweed extract @ 3oz/1000sqft

Application 2 (March)

> 4-3-6 @ 1/2lbN/1000sqft + 13-0-0 @ 1/2lbN/1000sqft (blood meal)
> Organic Micronutrient @ 3oz/1000sqft
> Seaweed extract @ 3oz/1000sqft

Application 3 (June)

> 9-3-5 @ 1/2lbN/1000sqft
> Gypsum @ 15lbs/1000sqft (applied during aerification while holes are open)
> Earthworm castings @ 10lbs/1000sqft (applied during aerification while holes are open)
> Granular humic acid @ 15lbs/1000sqft (applied during aerification while holes are open)

Application 4 (August)

> 4-3-6 @ 1/2lbN/1000sqft + 13-0-0 @ 1/2lbN/1000sqft (blood meal)
> Organic Micronutrient @ 3oz/1000sqft

Application 5 (October)

> 4-4-4 @ 1/2lbN/1000sqft
> Organic Micronutrient @ 3oz/1000sqft

Note the additional applications of blood meal (13-0-0) to add nitrogen. Bermudagrass is extremely nitrogen hungry and needs 4-5lbsN/1000/year to keep its color.

Making sense of vague reports

It's important to note that not all soil reports look the same. Some soil reports will not give you in depth soil recommendations that I usually complete for my clients or golf courses. This is because many labs do not have a soil agronomist on staff and it is costly for them to have one on staff. I recommend doing your homework and find out which lab in your area will give you great recommendations guidelines to follow. Just in case you have soil samples with vague soil recommendations I have come up with a few basic guidelines to follow.

A few general rules of thumb

1. High sodium, Mg, or potassium can be alleviated with calcium sulfate dihydrate (gypsum).
2. High levels of nutrients can be "freed" from the soil with organic fertilizers.
3. High pH (7.5 or greater) can be lowered with cotton seed meal or elemental sulfur.
4. Low pH (6 or lower) can be raised with calcium carbonate (lime).
5. The goal Cation Exchange capacity is 20. A low number on your soils report here is of no concern through a sound organic program.
6. The target organic matter percentage is 10%. Higher than this can create wet soils which can harbor root borne diseases and an undesirable surface to spend time on. Be sure to keep

this number in line with yearly soil reports and yearly cultivation practices.

Spreaders

The two main categories of spreader are the drop spreader and the rotary spreader. A drop spreader drops the product straight onto the target surface for precise control. A rotary spreader drops the product into a spinning unit that distributes the material outward onto the target surface. Both rotary spreaders and drop spreaders have pros and cons and it is important to know the value of each spreader as they can play a vital role in your program.

For most home use applications I would suggest using a rotary spreader as it requires less accuracy on your part. Depending on the bulk density of the product being applied a rotary spreader can spread up to ten times the width of a drop spreader. The larger spread width means less skips but also can be a downside around flower beds or non-target areas. Depending on how professional of a unit you purchase there are options to shield one side of rotary unit to apply around non target areas. There are also ways of retro-fitting a shield to protect non target areas but I don't recommend this method and I will talk more about this later. Wind can also be a factor depending on the density of the product you are applying. I would suggest avoiding applications of seed or light materials on windy days with a rotary spreader.

I would only suggest the use of a drop spreader if you have small areas of turf where you want to control exactly where the product is placed. For larger applications drop spreading becomes very tricky. With the width being as small as 18" (depending on unit width), spreading product on an entire lawn becomes difficult. However wind is not much a factor as drop spreaders are dropping the product very close to the ground. If you have a large lawn but also have many areas that require precise control consider the use of both drop and rotary spreaders.

Both spreader types come with an adjustment bar with numbers on it. The larger you set the number on the bar the larger the openings at the bottom of the spreader. Some fertilizer bags show suggested spreader settings to use if you are not interested in calibration of your spreader. These numbers should only be a starting point for calibration purposes. Using these numbers on the fertilizer bag can deliver results that may be far from your target rate.

Granular calibration

To properly calibrate you will need the following materials:

1. A spreader
2. A 100' tape measure or measuring wheel
3. Scale – A 20lb scale should be the smallest you should purchase
4. 5 gallon Bucket
5. Calculator
6. Notebook – This is to keep notes for future references

It's extremely important to keep in mind that the example below is for the "Single Direction" method. Please read both the Calibration section and Application section for a clear understanding of all the application methods before calibrating your spreader to the desired rate. Without knowing your application method you could be applying double or half the amount needed to your lawn.

Before calibration you will need to figure out how much product you will need to apply to your lawn. For this example let's pretend we are applying a fertilizer @ 1/2lb of N/1000sqft with the Single Direction method. But let's use our 4-4-4 product as an example. We know that this product contains 4% Nitrogen, 4% Phosphorus and 4% Potassium. Professional fertilizer product application amounts are described as a pound amount of a specific element per 1000sqft and the professional method is how I am going to train you. We will go over a quick and dirty calibration method later. Regardless of the element described the calibration procedure is exactly the same.

If we know that 4% of this product is nitrogen than we will use the following calculation to figure out how much product is needed to achieve our desired rate of 1/2lb of Nitrogen.

Take the number 100 (as in 100%: this is a constant) divide by 4 (as in 4%) = 25lbs of product. This means that for every 25lbs of 4-4-4 contains 1lb of nitrogen. But our target application rate is for 1/2lb. So we need to spread 12.5lbs of product per 1000sqft in order to apply 1/2lbN/1000sqft.

This poundage of product per 1000sqft is how some product labeled rates are explained. Note above that for my rates of earthworm castings, humic acid and gypsum they are explained as pounds of product per thousand. This just saves you a little math because you aren't trying to calibrate for a specific element like nitrogen. Labeled rates of some products could be described as one bag per 10,000sqft (1/10th of a bag per 1000sqft). If a suggested labeled rate is given to you as pounds of product for a given area then the first calculation is already done for you, you do not need to deal with the element percentages.

The first step in our calibration is to figure out how wide your application width is. For a drop spreader this number is always going to be the width of the spreader bin. A rotary spreader will differ depending on the product. To find out your width on a rotary spreader I suggest employing the help of a friend or family member.

1. First you will put a fair amount of product into the spreader. I like to fill the spreader up halfway. Find an area where you can spread your product that will not affect your lawn. A driveway is a good spot as long as the rain will not wash your product back onto your lawn.

2. Before you can begin measuring your application width, grab a few stones or sticks that you can line up to create a target. This will be your target on the right side of your throw and will run parallel to your walking path. Paint, chalk or even a scuff marking from your boot works well.

3. Your partner's job will be to stand on the left side of you and directly across from your right side target line that you have made. He or she will be your eyes on the left side when you are paying attention to the right side.

4. Adjust your spreader setting to level where you and your partner can easily see. Halfway between the lowest setting and highest setting should work.

5. You will now walk at your natural pace between your target on the right and your partner on the left applying the product for a couple of feet. Apply just enough to get a gauge on how wide you are throwing. While you are spreading make

sure the outer edge of your product application is hitting your right side target. Don't be so far away from your right target that only a few granules reach but not too close where you are throwing too much over your right target. You may want to try two or three times to get the feel of your throw width. At this same moment your partner on the left will be marking how far you are throwing on his or her side.

6. Once your partner has found a good edge of product on your left side he will either stand there or mark your edge. Again you partner will be marking where you are applying sufficient product, not out to the extreme edge with only a few granules of product have reached.

7. When you and your partner have decided that you have found the correct application width you can than measure the mark from your partner on the left and your target on the right. This is now your application width for that given product. Rarely will this ever change unless you walk at a faster or slower pace. This is why it is important to maintain your natural walking pace.

8. Record this number in your note book as the width associated with the product you are applying. Let's say you have found this application width to be 12 feet. It's a good idea to write this down in your notebook "4-4-4 application width of 12 feet".

9. Now that we know the spreader width we can now figure out how far we need to walk to apply the product in 1000sqft.

The calculation for this is as follows. 1000sqft (this number is constant) / 12ft (application width) = 83.33ft.

10. With this you can now measure out 83 feet (rounding down to keep things simple) with your tape measure or measuring wheel. You can also split this number in half and walk both ways if you wish. Make sure you have enough room to walk in a straight line. You now can clearly mark where to both open and close your spreader within this 83ft track you are making. Stones, sticks or a mark with your boot, all will suffice as long as you know exactly where to open and close.

11. You will now dump the remaining fertilizer from your spreader back into the bag. Make sure all of your fertilizer is completely out of the spreader. Once this is complete you can now use your bucket and scale to measure out fertilizer.

12. Zero out your scale by placing your bucket on the scale and adjusting its dial to read 0 while the bucket is on top of the scale.

13. Once the scale has been zeroed measure out 20lbs of your fertilizer. Our target application is 12.5lbs of product per thousand but measuring out 20lbs will assure your hopper does not get too light on product which can skew your calibrations. The 20lbs of product can now be dumped into the spreader hopper.

14. Adjust your spreader to the number given on the bag. If you do not have a recommended number than your first pass will be a complete guess as to what adjustment number to choose on your spreader.

15. After you have chosen a number you can now apply your fertilizer within the 83ft track you have marked off. Make sure you are walking in a straight line while applying and walking at your natural pace.

16. After application in your track is complete you can now dump your remaining fertilizer back into your bucket and weigh the remaining product. The remaining number you are looking for here is 7.5lbs (20lbs of product - 12.5lbs target). If the remainder is less than 7.5lbs you have spread too much, if the remainder is greater than 7.5lbs you have spread too little.

17. You now can adjust your spreader setting accordingly and re-measure out 20lbs in your bucket and start over. This may take up to 4 times to get a good spreader setting to use. But once you have found it you can then record this number in your notebook "4-4-4 fertilizer spreader setting is x for 1/2lb of N per 1000sqft."

For homeowner purposes calibrating your spreader for each product should be done every few years. For a landscaping company I would suggest once a year. On the golf course I calibrate before every application. But as long as you keep your spreader settings recorded you can use the same settings for the product throughout the year. These settings may change due to natural wear and tear of the spreader. Keeping a notebook handy with spreader settings is a good way to quickly check your calibration each year after your initial year of calibration.

The quick and dirty method

I realize that this type of professional calibration simply may not be possible for some homeowners due to the lack of off target area necessary to calibrate. For this I like to use the quick and dirty method. It's not the best but in a pinch will get you by. For this calibration type you need to know the square footage of your lawn which can be measured out with your measuring wheel or tape measure. Splitting your lawn up into smaller boxes can be useful in squared off lawns. It's helpful to draw out your lawn in an aerial map view and split your lawn up

If your lawn has an odd shape with no right angles than you can use a different method using averages. It's as simple as measuring widths from five equidistant spots and dividing by five to obtain the average width. Than find the average length measure from five equidistant spots and divide by five to get the average length. Multiply the average width by the average length to obtain the square footage of your lawn. The more equidistant spots you measure widths and lengths from will give you a more accurate square footage of your lawn.

Let's say you find that your lawn is 4500sqft and you are applying our 4-4-4 product from above. We already know that to apply 1/2lbN/1000sqft we need 12.5lbs of product (see math above). This means that the correct amount of product you need to apply to your lawn is 12.5 x 4.5 or 56lbs.

Now from here I like to measure out about 20lbs of product and choose a low setting on the spreader. You want to choose a lower setting because this is a complete guess as to the correct setting. The goal here is to apply your product in many different directions until you've used exactly 56lbs. It's important to keep tabs with your scale in between directions to know how many pounds you have applied. But let's say for the first direction you've chosen setting 5 and only used 15lbs of product. Quick math tells us you can either spread the product in 4 different directions and get 60lbs (close enough to 56lbs to call accurate) or gamble slightly and increase the setting for the next direction. Now from here you may choose to increase the setting to 8 on the spreader and try another direction and end up using another 27lbs. Well know you know you've used 42lbs and only need 14lbs more to get your perfect 56lbs total. We also know that on setting 5 you used 15lbs. We would then put the setting back to 5 and apply the product one more time in a different direction. Remember to keep weighing out product in between directions to know how much product you are applying and keep accurate notes for the next time you apply the product. Each time you apply the same product you can become more and more accurate to find the perfect setting number for your lawn.

Liquid calibration

To properly calibrate you will need the following materials:

1. 1-3 gallon sprayer (I personally use Field King lithium ion powered backpack sprayers for constant pressure)

2. A 100' tape measure or measuring wheel

3. Measuring cup of 64oz or greater

4. Chalk, flags or something to mark off 1000sqft

5. Calculator

6. Notebook – Keep notes for future references

Calibration of a liquid product can vary depending on the type of sprayer you are using. If you are using a simple 1 gallon sprayer use the following steps.

1. Fill your sprayer with exactly 128oz of water by using your measuring cup.
2. Mark out a 10'x10' square (100sqft) with your measuring tape.
3. Spray inside the square with a constant slow and steady back and forth motion.
4. Measure out the remainder of liquid within your sprayer.
5. For an example let's say you had a remainder of 106oz of water left within the sprayer. Subtract the 106oz of water

from 128 and find that you have sprayed 22oz within the 100sqft. This means that for a 1000sqft area you are going to use 220oz of solution. Now that we know we will be using 220oz of solution per 1000sqft this number shouldn't change as long as your nozzle stays the same and your application speed does not differ.

6. Taking the product seaweed extract we have chosen within our fertilizer plan we have a target rate of 3oz/1000sqft. This means that the 3oz needs to be sprayed evenly within the 220oz of solution we are applying.

- 128oz (oz. per sprayer tank) /220oz (total oz. used per 1000sqft) = .58
  So each sprayer filled completely with 1 gallon of water can cover 580sqft (.58x1000)
- 3oz (rate per 1000sqft) * .58 = 1.74

So in order to apply this product at 3oz per 1000sqft using our 1 gallon sprayer you would need 1.74oz of seaweed per tank. This tank would then be able to cover 580sqft at the same application speed you calibrated at.

This small tank is only suggested for small areas and usually better for applying insect or disease products. If you would like to do an entire lawn with a liquid fertilizer like the same seaweed product at 3oz/1000sq ft. I would suggest a larger backpack sprayer like the Field King lithium ion or a hose proportioner like a Chapin hose end sprayer found on amazon. With a hose end sprayer I would use the same calibration technique as my quick and dirty granular method above. Hose spray the lawn in as many directions as possible until the target application amount has been achieved.

Conversions for granular products

Linear

      1 foot = 12 inches

      1 yard = 3 feet

      1 meter = 3.281 feet

      1 meter = 1.094 yards

Square

      1 sq. ft. = 144 sq. inches

      1 sq. yard = 9 sq. feet

      1 acre = 43,560 sq. ft. = 4,840 sq. yards = 0.405 hectares

Rates

      1 lb./1000 sq. ft. = 43.6 lb./acre

      100 lb./acre = 2.5 lb./1000 sq. feet

Weights

      1 ounce = 28.35 grams

      1 pound = 16 ounces = 453.5 grams

      1 ton = 2000 pounds

      1 kilogram = 2.205 pounds = 1000 grams

Application

In the calibration section we went over the basic principle of application width. In order to teach proper application techniques I have created another term I use for teaching called line width. It's important to know the difference so these terms do not become confused.

Application width – The total width of the throw for the product you are applying. In the calibration section our example was 12ft.

Line width – The width between each walking pass you make with your spreader.

Line width can differ depending on the application technique chosen. For two of the application techniques the application width and the line width are the same but for one method the line width is only half of the application width. I will go into the details on how this works while I explain each method.

Rotary spreader

There are 3 different ways to apply product out of a rotary spreader. The application techniques are two direction, throw to pass, and single direction. Other people may name them different but these are the names I use for my teaching purposes. Both Two Direction and Throw Back to Pass I use on a normal basis. Single Direction I normally would not suggest using. It's the fastest of the three methods but also the least precise and hard to avoid skips and overlaps. Regardless of your application technique applying products should always be done in strait lines.

The Two Direction method is just like it sounds, applying your product in two directions. For the Two Direction method you will need to calibrate your fertilizer product for half of the amount of your desired rate. This is because you are applying the product on your lawn twice. So instead of our example rate of 12.5lbs of product per 1000sqft (in the calibration section) the number now would be 6.25lbs of product per 1000sqft. Once you have the correct calibration for your product you can than begin applying. With Two Direction you are using the total spread width of your spreader. The application width and the line width are the same. For example if your application width is 12 feet than your line width is 12ft wide as well. After your first pass you will move over 12 feet and start your second pass going in the opposite direction. I would not suggest however to literally measure your application lines on every pass. Just simply watch the outer edge of your product's dispersal and make mental notes as to where you should be throwing on your next pass. Once you have completed the lawn to its entirety you will do it all over again in a direction that's perpendicular to your first. If your first set of lines was lengthwise your next set will be widthwise. If you first chose a diagonal path than an opposite diagonal path should be chosen on your second set of application lines. Making two directions like this will assure even coverage of your product.

Throw Back to Pass is similar to Two Direction in that you will also have to calibrate to half of your desired amount. But also different to two direction because you will be applying the product so it overlaps back to the walking path of your previous pass. So this means when choosing the Throw Back to pass method your line width is only half of your application width. This is because you are throwing your product back to the middle of your last line, or throwing back to your last walking path. Instead of paying attention to where the outer edge of your fertilizer is throwing you will be making sure that the fertilizer is throwing into your last walking path. When using this method you will actually start and end your application on the very edge of the lawn. This means that you will be throwing product outside of your target area.

Now with that being said I did briefly touch base earlier on a way to retro-fit a directional blocker to your spreader. This will prohibit product from being thrown into non target areas. This can easily be done by either zip tying a board or piece of cardboard to one side of the spreader which blocks the throw to one side but It's important to know what the downsides of this are. When blocking one side of the rotary spreader you are essentially taking fertilizer that was meant to be evenly thrown several feet outward and getting it to fall strait down. This means that where it does fall the application rate will be extremely heavy. It's not a great thing to do when applying fertilizer because this means that all your outward edges you did use the blocker on are going to be over fertilized. This will eventually cause problems with thatch and an overabundance of organic material within these edges. That being said some expensive professional models accommodate for this problem allow you to lower the rate within this area by closing some of the holes at the bottom of the spreader. In this case this becomes a great tool to use.

Lastly the technique of Single Direction is exactly the same as Two Direction but just as the name suggests you are only applying in one direction. This type of application requires you to calibrate your spreader to the full desired amount of 12.5lbs/1000sqft. It is the quickest way to apply any product but I would not suggest using this method as it can result in many skips and overlaps.

No matter your application technique I would suggest having a friend or family member help to mark where you need to walk on each next pass. He or she will stand on the on one side of the lawn facing toward you. As you apply the product he or she will stand where your next pass needs to be. As you turn around at the end of your line you will get a clear visual on where to walk. This can serve as training wheels until you become confident enough to walk in strait lines without skipping or overlapping your product. If you do not have a partner available consider dropping a hat, using marking flags or utilizing a dew covered morning. Most turf care professionals are afraid of applying fertilizers in dew as most fertilizers have a high burn potential. As another benefit to organic fertilizers you have the luxury of taking advantage of the dew and applying without any risk of burn. This will allow you to see your tracks easily and know exactly where your next pass needs to be.

I prefer flip flopping a two directional method with the Throw to pass method. One application would be done in a Two Direction fashion whereas the next would be done with Throw to Pass. Also switch up the direction in which you start your applications. Follow the pictures below for examples for application techniques.

Throw to pass

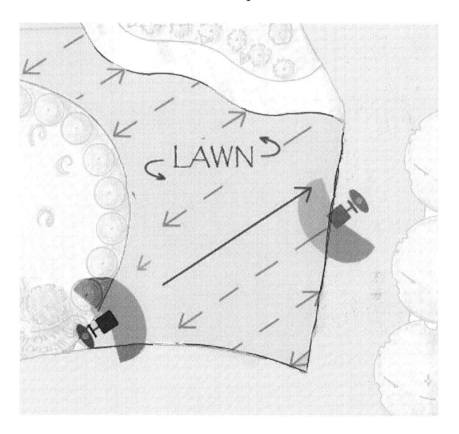

For training purposes I have chosen a particularly odd shaped lawn. With this shape and a throw to pass method there will be significant fertilizer that will be applied outside the target zone. Not an environmental concern with organic products but still wasting money. Notice the direction I have chosen will not change once application has started no matter the shape of the lawn. This is very important to maintain a consistent application rate. Also you can see that each application pass throws to the middle of your walk path on the previous line

Two Direction

For the two direction method I have chosen the same diagonal pattern but notice that the passes are now double the distance between them when compared to throw to pass. It will essentially give you the same result but it's always a good idea to change your direction each time you apply to assure uniformity throughout the season.

Drop spreader

If you own a drop spreader I would highly suggest the purchase of marking flags for proper application. By using these flags at the start of each pass you can mark the outside of your spreader so you know exactly where to walk on each pass. This will minimize your skips and overlaps. Cool season grasses may allow you to apply without marking flags. The soft texture of the grass may be enough to show you the tire marks of each pass. Remember to apply to the inside edge of your tire marks. The reason is that the outside edge of your spreader bucket does not extend to the outside edge of your tire marks.

For application with a drop spreader I would suggest only using the Two Direction method (as seen in the picture). With this method you can use the same tactics as you would with a rotary spreader. Make sure you calibrate for half of your target rate as you will be going over the lawn twice. The only difference is your application width is the width of your spreader bucket. This will never change no matter your product.

Using the Single Pass method with a drop spreader makes it almost impossible to apply your product perfectly while using a drop spreader. A line that's even an inch off can cause a skip or an overlap. For this reason I would avoid using this method entirely. Also using a throw to pass method can become confusing. With a drop spreader you are moving over on each pass only half the width of your spreader which is so little that you can easily get side tracked and start applying using the Single Pass without noticing.

Liquid application
I like to apply my liquids in a smooth back and forth motion and moving backward at a consistent pace. Moving backward will stop you from walking through your application. Overlaps and skips are pretty hard to avoid. The easiest way to see your liquids is to spray either early in the morning where dew is present.

WATERING

Establishment

For the most part watering during any type of establishment whether it's starting a new lawn from seed, sprigs, sod or even over seeding the general rule of thumb is to keep the soil moist until it's either germinated, the sprigs have started to spread, or the sod has knitted its roots into the soil. After that step you can cut the water back to watering a few hours before sunrise once per day. Keeping the top of the soil moist longer than this period can increase the risk of diseases and pests. Usually this period lasts less than 14 days.

At establishment it is very important to have an automated system in place for watering. Whether that be a pre-installed irrigation system or sprinklers set up on timers that you can rotate throughout the day to keep the entire lawn moist. Hand watering never works as well because it takes quite a bit of effort to stay on time and devote the time to stay outside watering your lawn. More often than not it's an over commitment to think you can stay on schedule with hand watering until your lawn is past the establishment stage.

If you have a really large lawn then purchasing a few hoses and sprinklers may not seem like it's worth it but it can cut down on a lot of extra work involved. If purchasing the proper amount of watering equipment needed seems expensive to you than you can split your establishment areas. Start your new turf on the front lawn, two weeks later do the back. Usually after two weeks either your seeds have germinated and started to grow grass or your sprigs have rooted in.

Maintenance

To maintain a sustainable water conscious lawn there are a few practices that you have to learn and start to implement. Depending on where you live in the world usually the amount of rainfall you receive will not sustain your lawn with adequate amounts of moisture without supplemental watering. The proper watering techniques alone will help you with a whole host of problems such as diseases, weeds and other pests and actually keep your grass greener. These watering basics will also help you save money on your water bill. Most lawns in the world waste hundreds of gallons of water due to improper scheduling and timing alone.

A healthy lawn that is watered properly with a deep and infrequent method has minimal disease, weed and insect problems. Golf courses which can go through over 600,000 gallons per night know this principle better than anybody. Where water costs on some golf courses are in the thousands of dollars per day, it pays to know how and when and how to water properly.

As a general rule of thumb a lawn needs about 1" of water per week to survive. This can be in combination with rainfall so I suggest purchasing a rain gauge and or a rain shutoff switch if you have an irrigation system already in place. A rainfall of ½" can be enough for you to turn off your irrigation sprinklers or forego hand watering for few days. With a rainfall of 1" or more I like to span out my next watering to 3 days or more after, keeping a close eye for dry spots. When dry spots do start to show quickly after a significant rain event address them with a hose only. Turning on your entire irrigation system after a rainfall because of one dry spot is most likely going to keep the rest of your lawn too wet. By only watering these dry spots you will encourage deep roots by letting the rest of your lawn dry naturally. Once a few days after a rain event has passed and you notice a bit more dry spots than you'd like to handle with a hose feel free and run a full irrigation cycle to correct moisture in the soil immediately. Than you can feel free to turn the timer back on and continue to water on your normal days per week.

Without rainfall plan on your goal being only to water your lawn 2-4 times per week but deeply enough to water the entire root zone. This deep watering can be checked with a shovel by digging to a depth of 6" anytime in the morning of your watering. If your lawn is wet all the way down to 6" you've got a sufficient amount of water to hold you over for a few days. Just remember to check daily in the heat of the day for hot spots. Repeat the same process of hand watering hot spots when they show. If you find yourself hand watering the same exact spots time after time consider the use of a wetting agent (an additive to reduce surface tension of water in order to yield improved penetration of water). You can apply this with a sprayer attachment like the Chapin hose end sprayer to a hose to the affected areas and will help water penetrate these hydrophobic spots easier. Prior to watering these dry spots, be sure to not walk on them as this will break the cells of the blades of grass and create dead spots in the shape of your footprint.

The best time of day to water is a few hours before sunrise. This will give your water sufficient time to soak into the root zone and not be evaporated by the sun. Of course waking up at this time to hand water your lawn is not something you need to be doing either. If you do not have an automatic irrigation system I would advise you purchase a few sprinklers with timers and rotate them daily in order to get the coverage needed to water your lawn properly throughout the week. This can be done relatively inexpensive depending on the size of your lawn. An impact type sprinkler head would normally be the best option. For a timer something from Orbit is always a good option for a home owner.

I always advise against watering early in the evening. Watering early in the evening causes your lawn to stay wet throughout the night. This damp upper profile creates an environment favorable for diseases and algae to establish themselves in your lawn.

Of course watering deeply does sometimes require a bit of strategy depending on your soil type. Some soil types do not accept water as fast as others, so you may have to split up your watering timings. For the most part automatic systems apply water faster than the soil can accept so you may have to split up your watering. For example if you have found that 25 minutes a night 3 times a week is sufficient then you may want to water 12 minutes wait an hour and then run another 12 minute cycle in order to avoid any run off and waste money on water. If you have a simple hose set up to a sprinkler you can find simple valve timers that attach onto the hose and allow for a simple scheduling solution.

Some people will tell you to measure your output of water each night by putting out a series of cans or cups and taking measurement. This is a total waste of time. Not once in my career have I felt the need to do this. Lawns have natural wet spots and dry spots due to different aggregate sizes being concentrated in certain areas. It's impossible to get a lawn that has exactly the same soil in every square foot. It's meaningless to know you are putting out the exact amount of water across your lawn if your lawn does not have exactly the same soil throughout it. With time you will begin to know your lawn dry spots and wet spots and adjust times and move sprinklers accordingly. In this respect it's as much of an art as it is a science. Seeing what is becoming dry and feeling soil moisture with your fingers are the best two weapons you can use when implementing proper watering techniques.

For example if I know my grass is normally being watered every other night I will be looking for dry spots on the second day. By keeping an eye on your lawn you can quickly gauge whether or not your lawn needs more water or less. Dry spots can be quickly identified by their grey dull color on warm season grasses and purple blackish color on cool season. Dry plants will also show signs of wilt and grass blades will actually shrivel up and close in an attempt to conserve water. Do not let these go un-noticed, making haste can save these spots from turning brown and dying back. Dry spots like this that are watered immediately will suffer no additional progression of discoloration and can recover quickly. However if left unnoticed and the dry spot then turns brown it will take up to several weeks to fully recover even after heavy watering. These spots can also open the door for weed breakthrough to occur.

It is important to note to never mow your lawn when you have dry spots like these. Mowing over grass that lacks water can cause the grass to die back to the soil surface. Instead take the time and watering these spots deeply with a hose. Fully drenching the soil once and then again 5 minutes later. This will aid water percolation when your soil is hydrophobic due to its dry condition. After you have watered all of your spots heavily you may mow the following day. Worst case scenario skipping a mowing for a day or two and slightly scalping your grass is far better than mowing over dry spots and creating dead spots on your lawn.

Installing automated irrigation

Watering with a properly installed automated irrigation system assures even coverage of your watering and will save many hours outside hand watering or moving sprinklers on hoses around. The initial cost of installation may seem a bit pricey at first but in the long run will prove to save money on water by watering at the optimal times of day. Also consider the addition of a rain shutoff switch, which will shut down your irrigation system if you receive rainfall while away on vacation or while you sleep at night.

All homeowner irrigation systems are controlled by valves. These valves usually control up to 10 or more irrigation heads. The combined area of each of the heads that the valve controls is called a zone. Once the valve is turned on water passes into the pipes and turns on the sprinkler heads. This means that there is no static water pressure after the zone in the irrigation piping. The only water that is under static pressure is the water before the valves. So if you accidentally pierce the piping or head when aerating your lawn you will not see the damage until you turn on the valve or zone associated with that section.

When choosing zones, small areas in your lawn are usually split apart from larger ones. The reasoning is that small areas are usually reserved for a smaller sprinkler heads such as mist head or a dancing rain head. This smaller areas use smaller heads in order to not waste water thrown into non target areas. Adjustments of a mist head usually is as simple as purchasing a nozzle for the correct angle needed where dancing rain heads are adjusted from the top of the head with a small tool.

Larger areas are reserved for rotor heads. Rotor heads throw water much further than mister heads and move in a back and forth motion to assure good coverage. Adjustment of rotor heads can be trickier than a mister head. Rotor heads turn at a set pace chosen from the manufacturer, so water application rates vary depending on the degree the rotor head is adjusted for and the nozzle setup chosen (this usually depends on the size of the area). For example say you have two rotor heads on the same zone, one is adjusted for a half circle throw at 180 degrees and one is set for a full circle throw at 360. The grass in front of the half circle rotor will receive twice as much water as the 360 degree throw with the same nozzle. Why? Because it may take 1 minute for a rotary head to make a full circle where it only would take 30 seconds for a half circle head to throw 180 degrees. In other words in one minute a half circle head would make two full sweeps over the grass while a full circle head adjustment would only make one full sweep. Knowing this basic principle your irrigation company should install all part circle rotors with low flow nozzle setups.

Secondly it's quite difficult to get your mist heads and rotor heads to put out the same gallons of water per minute. Mist heads usually put out far less gallons of water per minute then a rotor head. For that reason I would never pair mist head with rotor heads on the same zone. This is because your mister heads will have to run for more time than your rotor heads to achieve equal coverage. If the company you have chosen has proposed such a setup, they might have good reason ask your chosen irrigation company if they could walk you through the reasoning if they have paired these two types of heads within the same zone.

If your irrigation system is already installed and you have part circle rotor heads paired with full circle rotors or rotors matched with mist heads it may not be possible to convert your lawn without redoing the entire installation. In this case it may be a good idea to call an irrigation specialist for a consultation of what they can do to fix the problem.

MOWING

Mower types

Each type of lawn mower has its own benefits. Golf courses for example can have 6 or more completely different types of mowers suited to different jobs throughout the course. Some are better than others at certain tasks. Consider a good mower as an investment that should not be made in haste. Choosing the correct type can save you thousands of dollars and hundreds of hours of work per year. It could be that the least inexpensive type fits your lawn and budget best or you need a slightly more expensive model in order to mow your large lawn faster. In most cases the quality of cut won't differ from a $300 push mower to a $50,000 professional riding mower. The main difference is speed and ease of work load. An expensive unit will have more power and torque giving it abilities of mowing through your lawn at a faster pace while still giving you a great cut.

Rotary push lawn mower

Rotary push mowers are powered by either gas or electricity. Push rotary mowers are usually my choice for smaller areas in the lawn, or even a choice for the full work load as long as the lawn is small. For example on most golf courses these are used around tight spots that riding mowers can't maneuver very easily. They can be quite heavy to push, for this reason some do come with motorized wheels. These are more expensive models and it has been my experience that this feature always ends up breaking at some point or another regardless of the quality of unit. I have purchased $700 professional line self-propelled rotary units and the drive motors still break. Of course you can still run the mower if it does break, you will just have to push the unit, but it will be heavier than other non-self-propelled models because of the weight of the extra motors.

Most models come with a bag already attached, be sure to know if your model can do both bagging and mulching. Bagging can have its purpose and can be used when you want to clean up leaves or verticutting material but should not be used every time.

My recommendation – If you must have a self-propelled walk unit than look into Lawn Boy. Lawn Boy is Toro's homeowner lawn care division, and Toro is a company I use for basically everything on my golf courses and recommend to professionals. Lawn boy models can start out cheap and work their way up to a higher end models. Most models are self-propelled, but their systems are a cheap enough fix if anything should go wrong. If you don't need the motorized self propelled drive than look into models from Honda. They are inexpensive and will last. With either choice one key feature you need to compare is a mower's torque output. Higher priced models have more torque to cut through thick grass at a faster pace. If you're a landscaping company or a homeowner that needs the best, purchase a mower from **Exmark or Toro**. Be warned, it is commercial quality so expect commercial prices.

Riding mowers (ride-on mowers)

If you have a larger lawn or don't like the thought of pushing a mower around for an hour or so look into something that you can ride on. Within the riding mower category you have standing riders (more for commercial use) and riders that you sit down on which are more for residential use. Keep in mind if you have trees or areas you won't be able to maneuver properly you will either have to purchase a weed trimmer or push mower to reach these areas. Again make sure your riding mower isn't pigeon holed into bagging clippings every time it mows. Mulching is what you want to do in most cases so make sure your unit can do both.

I'd suggest **Exmark for the professionals here** but unfortunately for a homeowner the prices are very high. So in most cases something from **Husqvarna** is a great brand for the weekend warrior. They offer zero turn which means they turn from the rear wheels and can literally turn in their own footprint. The higher end models offer things like striping kits which makes mowing professional stripes in your lawn an easy thing to do.

Tractor lawn mowers

Tractor type solutions can often times be the most expensive. You would usually purchase a separate tractor such as a **Kubota** or John Deere and have several attachments such as a **brush mower, rotary grass unit, verti-cutting unit, and aerifying unit** to be used from the PTO drive off from the back of the tractor. I would advise against this purchase unless you have a large field area to maintain or would like to tackle the job of aeration and verti-cutting on your own lawn. Having a tractor on your property does have its benefits such as plowing snow and if you have a long dirt driveway you can buy a **box blade** and do yearly leveling yourself. You can also purchase several other attachments such as a **soil auger** for planting trees, or a **backhoe** for other digging applications such as drainage or removal of smaller stumps. If you are a landscaping company looking for the ultimate in power and versatility the John Deere 5065e is far and away the best tractor I have used on my properties. Enough power to easily pull 5 yards of wet sand up a steep gradient and small enough to operate in tighter situations.

Reel mowers

There are two types of reel mowers. One of which in my opinion is not feasible for most homeowner's situations because of its price and cost of maintenance and the other is very cheap and can be suitable for very small lawn applications. It is important to note however that reel mowers have trouble cutting grass and weeds past 1.5". It doesn't matter how expensive the model, it's just the way the cutting unit is designed. This short height goes against many principles of organic lawn care. For this reason and a few others I will go over why I usually suggest against the purchase.

The first reel type mower is one that is used mostly on golf courses and cost more than $50,000 for a 100" width fairway unit and $8500 for a 21" walk behind greens mower. Even if you were to buy a smaller used unit from a golf course or ball park for a reasonable price the knowledge needed to maintain this type of mower is quite immense. Simply sharpening the reels you need a special grinding unit that you most likely will not find anywhere but a golf course or ball park. Some course mechanics may let you drop off your unit to them to sharpen after hours but depending on the golf course policies it still might not be possible. If anything goes wrong with the unit again you would need to employ the help of somebody with knowledge of units like a golf course mechanic. Maintenance alone would be much more expensive and stressful then simply buying a rotary unit.

The second type of reel mower is a **manual push mower**. These do not have a motor and are powered by you pushing it and gearing within the wheel mechanism. These types are ok to use when your lawn is maintained at low cutting heights and you have a small lawn. These units are not meant for extremely thick grass and you will find have trouble cutting weeds. Also proper sharpening of these units may be tough to complete on your own as the reel needs to be spun against a grinding stone at high speeds. These work best on Bermuda, Paspalum and Zoysia. Cool season grasses that are being cut with a unit such as this may require a double cut in order to achieve acceptable results. More on double cutting later.

Electric mowers

An electric mower are inexpensive to operate and relatively easy to maintain. Most of the machines described above today come in electric models, either corded or cordless lithium ion battery powered. They are well worth considering as a quiet and eco-friendly choice. Some models provided by Snapper can last up to 45minutes on a single charge. I have not personally used any electric mowers but I have heard good things from our landscaping crews on some of my golf courses.

Another interesting new type of electric mower that has become available within the last few years are automated **robotic mowers**. They work similarly to automatic robotic vacuum cleaners or pool cleaners. I however have not had any experience with such mowers. From what I have researched, they are still a bit too unreliable to consider as a viable option. If you were to buy this type of mower I would strongly suggest getting to know the manufacturer's warranty and the amount of money you can expect to spend on services and wear and tear parts.

Hover mowers

These mowers are motorized with a rotary blade, but they have no wheels. Instead, they float above the ground on a cushion of air. They are especially useful for steep hills or slopes, where regular mowers would slip or even be dangerous to use. Lots of the same applications used for trimmers can be instead used with a hover mower. The price for a good hover mower however can be about double the cost of a good trimmer, but hover mowers can get lawn trimming done about twice as fast. Keep in mind however that hover mowers cannot mow through tall field type grass or brush. If you have these types of jobs to complete on your property I would suggest going with a trimming machine to complete all of your tasks.

My recommendation – Purchase a model from **Husqvarna**. They are sold in many places in the United States including Amazon so it is easy to find replacement parts if needed. Also opt for blades instead of trimmer line if given the choice. These will give you a cleaner cut and it will become easier to cut through taller grass. Also if you are using hover mowers on warm season grasses be aware that hover mowers will eventually hover on the thatch layer of your grass rather than the soil. This will cause the thatch layer of these areas to build faster than the areas you maintain with a mower and may require extra verticutting and or aerifying.

Trimmers

Trimmers can complete various tasks on your property. By purchasing the proper attachments you can clear brush, limb trees, edge your driveway and flower beds, cut down tall grass and cut lawn areas where your mower cannot reach. For gas powered trimmers I recommend any from Husqvarna, Echo, Stihl or Redmax. All of these companies sell professional grade models that have attachments sold separately to expand the use of your trimmers work load.

Electric trimmers come in both corded and cordless lithium powered models. If you already own the Dewalt flex-volt line their trimmer is superb. The battery is interchangeable with all Dewalt 20v tools and very powerful. All of my woodworking tools and landscape tools I use around the house are Dewalt so I can speak for their quality. If you want to purchase a corded trimmer I would go with a model from Toro. The great benefit here is trimming without all the noise.

The basics of mowing

Mowing is one of the most important maintenance duties to your lawn. Implementing good mowing practices alone can improve the look of your lawn within a matter of minutes. Mowing performed at the correct height and frequency is essential to the health and density of your turf stand. Clipping the proper amount of leaf material induces plants to form new sprouts, increasing stand density. A dense healthy lawn can withstand more pest pressure and needs fewer pest control inputs. Dense turf also helps prevent soil erosion, weed germination and helps prevent evapotranspiration (loss of soil moisture).

Height of Cut

Turf grasses are well adapted to frequent mowing, but mowing too short will reduce the vigor of the plants by reducing their ability to manufacture ATP (the food energy created by your grass through photosynthesis). Also, there is a direct relationship between cutting height and root mass. Lowering the mowing height will reduce the length and density of your root system. This restricts the ability of the plant to absorb water and nutrients and increases the amount of water needed to maintain your lawn. After many field trials, recommendations for mowing height in recent years have steadily increased. Current standards suggest between 2 and 3.75 inches (much lower for Paspalum and Bermuda varieties) depending on the species of grass. Simply put the higher the cut the more stress tolerant the grass. With more stress tolerances your plant can naturally defend itself against insects and diseases. This is especially important during the heat of summer. Taller grass plants with higher density have a profound shading effect on the soil surface, which reduces germination of weed seeds and slows evapotranspiration. Be sure to see the grass types section within this book to get an exact height suggestion depending on your grass species.

Mowing Frequency

A general rule of thumb is not to remove more than one-third of the total leaf surface when mowing your lawn. This may require mowing every four to five days during periods of rapid growth such as the spring and summer time when your soil microbes are becoming active. If you mow more than 1/3 your grass plant at any one time you risk scalping your grass. Scalping can be indicated by a white haze on the tops of your grass that show several hours or the day after mowing has been completed. Scalping can cause disease, weak spots allow weeds to germinate. Most home owners I see actually do scalp their lawns on a regular basis. This constant stress on turf is the main reason why most lawns cannot compete with weed encroachment and suffer from disease and insects.

The only time I ever would suggest scalping your grass is prior to overseeding or if you have Bermudagrass or Paspalum. During overseeding this will allow sunlight to reach your seeds and allow for a good yield on your crop. For Bermuda and Paspalum a target mowing height of 1-1.5" during the summer months is considered best practice to keep your lawns looking their best for fall-spring months.

Dealing with clippings

I am not a fan of bagging clippings. If you are mowing your lawn often enough the amount of clippings on your lawn will be minimal. If however you wait too long between mowing you will get a mess of clippings on top of your grass. In this case excessive accumulation of clippings may smother the turf and should be raked into your lawn's canopy.

Mowing without a bag also returns nutrients and organic matter back into the soil. A common misconception is that clippings left on the lawn will promote thatch buildup. This is not true. Clippings do not make significant contributions to thatch buildup. Grass clippings are mostly made up of water and nutrients which break down rapidly. To accommodate this practice, many mowers often come with mulching blades which break down the grass clippings into even smaller pieces and evenly distribute them back into the turf surface.

Some of my clients do try to insist on bagging clippings for compost purposes. It's an old gardener's trick and a silly process to begin with. You're either taking nutrients from the grass in order to either put them back on the grass in compost form or you're using that compost to spread them out within their flower beds. So it's either an extra step that's not needed or it's robbing Peter to pay Paul. But for the sake of argument let's say you are bagging your clippings for compost purposes. An important concept for composting is to create the correct carbon to nitrogen ratio within the pile. Many experts suggest an ideal ratio of 30:1 carbon to nitrogen for best compost results. This ratio can be as complex but to keep it simple grass clippings are relatively high in nitrogen, with an approximate 13:1 ratio for green clippings. Combining or layering grass clippings with tree leaves, straw, soil or other materials considered to have a high carbon content will be an effective choice for creating that perfect ratio.

I would advise against using fresh grass clippings for mulch in ornamental or vegetable gardens. Grass clippings piled on too heavily can create an impermeable layer for water to percolate through.

You can also mulch tree leaves into your soil or cut and bag tree leaves that to be used for compost. Be careful not to mow/mulch so many leaves back into your lawn that you are shading out your turf stand. I have read studies have evaluated the effects of mowing tree leaves into lawns. In these studies, up to 6 inches of various types of tree leaves were mowed into lawns. No adverse effects were detected on the lawns. Reports from professional turf managers who have been practicing this technique on golf courses and commercial turf have been positive. And that's great for them but it's absolutely not what I have found. Normally any parts of my golf courses covered by too much leaf material always have trouble growing extremely dense. This is due to the simple fact that the leaves are shading out the turf canopy from getting the proper sunlight needed. So by all means you can try it, but I don't consider this as a valuable trick of the trade.

Sharpening blades

The key to a quality cut with any style mower is to use a sharp, well-adjusted mower. Dull, poorly adjusted equipment tears rather than cuts the grass, leaving a ready site for disease invasion and giving the lawn a frayed, brownish look.

One of the most important factors in maintaining glowing green grass worthy of televised PGA Tour tournaments is maintaining razor sharp blades. During major tournaments my mechanics work constantly to ensure blades are as sharp as they can be. The sharper the blades the healthier the grass.

An easy way to assure you are always using a fresh set of sharp blades is to purchase an extra mower blade for your machine. Always keep your spare blade sharp so that when you have to switch it's done so quickly and easily. The exact frequency of changing the blade is up to you. On golf courses, mower blades are either sharpened, replaced or checked daily. For a home owner however twice a season should suffice unless you are hitting lots of tree roots, branches or other non-grass materials with your mower. For best results, mow when the turf is dry; this will also eliminate clippings clumping up on you lawn.

Striping your lawn

The quickest way to make any lawn or turf plot look better and hide imperfections is to stripe your grass. Stripes on turf grass are actually caused by a roller attached to a mower bending the grass. This bending does not hurt the grass, it simply pushes it down slightly. Grass bent toward you appears darker, as grass bent away appears lighter in color. I have always taught the workers on my golf courses the straighter your stripe lines, the better the grass looks. For perfect stripes however, it requires a lot of practice. The principle and technique of striping is quite easy, but becoming good at it requires some time behind a mower.

Most residentially available mowers do not come with a striping roller attached. On professional mowers the striping roller is either the drive roller for walk behind reel mowers, or acts as the wheels of each cutting unit on a professional riding mower. Normally for residentially available mowers however there are no rollers attached. Instead the mower has only wheels unless the mower states "striping kit attached". The good news is that striping kits can be purchased nowadays for any mower. It's a great attachment to grab if you want your lawn to have that wow factor.

For all beginners looking to mow their first stripes I like to tell people to put on a baseball cap first. Sounds silly at the moment but it will all make sense when you start. The first pass of your mower should be splitting the lawn into two sides. On this first pass you are going to choose a direction. There are 4 different directions to mow your lawn in. The 4 directions are chosen by the hands of a clock. If 12oclock is your back yard and 6oclock is your front you can create the following directions. 12 to 6 (front to back), 3 to 9 (side to side), 2 to 8 (diagonal) and 4 to 10 (diagonal). Mow one direction each time you mow in this order and repeat once you are through the sequence. If you want your lawn to look really nice for an event or get together you can double cut your lawn in two directions 12 to 6 and 3 to 9 or 2 to 8 and 4 to 10. This will take on a checker boarding effect as long as your mower is equipped with a striper. This assures that each time you mow your lawn the direction will be different than the last time. It can be handy to keep a log to keep track of your mowing directions.

First step is to do a quick walk through first just to make sure you are not going to hit any debris while mowing. With your direction now chosen now you will pick a target to keep looking at while mowing your first pass. The important thing about this target is that it should be high enough off the ground to be able to see the entire time you are mowing your first line. The reasoning behind this is that if there are any dips or low spots in your lawn you will lose sight of your target if it's not high enough. Once your target is chosen you're going to use your cap as a training wheels to keep you on track. Your target should be directly in the middle of the curvature of your hat brim.

The brim of the hat will help you keep your head straight and keep focused on the target. Your peripheral vision should be used here in order not to hit any debris or obstacles on your lawn. Once your first line is complete you are going to turn around and mow your second line. Let's mow the left side of the lawn first for training purposes. Take your time in lining up the deck of the mower so it has a proper 3-4" of overlap. The amount of overlap here is just in what you are comfortable with. I tell my new operators on my golf course to overlap more at first until they feel comfortable just so they don't have any skips while mowing. Once you are lined up for your next pass you are no longer going to look for a target outside of your lawn, your target will be the left side edge of the first pass that you just completed. In case of undulations and cannot see the end of your first line, look down at the right side of the line as far as you can. Never look directly down at the mower blade as this will always cause curved lines or lines with lots of quick correction zig zags. Once your second line is completed turn around again and keep mowing with the same method. Once you have completed the left side you can than walk or ride back to the middle and now continue to cut the right side of the lawn in the same fashion. Remember, you will always be mowing against a dark line not a light line so remember to continue the second half of the lawn in the correct direction. The second half of the lawn will be started in the opposite direction of your first mowing line. If you start the mowing the second half in the wrong direction you will end up with the middle of your lawn having a light colored stripe that is double width. Once you are done both sides of your lawn you can now do a cleanup pass. Which is a perimeter run of your lawn that you will mow in order to catch all the grass you have missed on the edges of your lawn.

Lastly if there is an obstacle in your lawn such as a tree never start your first pass aiming toward it. You always want the first pass to be an uninterrupted line from one side to the other. If you were to aim for the obstacle in the middle of your lawn as the first pass it will be very hard to keep that line strait once you maneuver around the obstacle. Once you are done all your stripes you then can return back to the obstacle by driving or walking down a light colored stripe (grass that is bent away from you) as to not disturb the look of your lawn. Once you have reached your obstacle mow its perimeter with one cleanup pass. Once complete drive away down a light colored stripe as to not create addition tire marks on your lawn.

I recommend practicing striping your lawn regularly. It may take some time to master but being able to walk in strait lines will help you in both mowing and product applications such as fertilizers. Remember that in order to mow bold stripes find out if your mower comes with a striping kit or if you can purchase one separate. Many companies offer after-market striping kits that can bolt on to many mowers. These will give you that baseball field or golf course look. The bolder the striping the more you can hide imperfections in your lawn.

The height of your grass, species of grass and angle of the sun of your grass also play a role in the boldness of your stripes. The higher the cut, the bolder the stripe. Reason being is that there is more grass to bend over. Some warm season grasses such as St. Augustine and Centipede grass simply will not stripe because of the texture and growth pattern. You will notice that throughout the day the striping of your grass will change its look or intensity as the sun changes its position in the sky.

CULTIVATION

Aeration

Aeration is the act of removing existing material from your lawn via the use of a machine that pulls hollow cores out of the soil profile. The end result is small holes into your lawn that are needed in order to add air to the root zone of the plant, increase microbial activity, reduce thatch, reduce compaction and increase water percolation efficiency. For the purposes of lawn care you should only be using core aeration or tines that will produce soil cores as opposed to the use of solid tines which do not pull material out of the soil profile. Core aeration has a much more dramatic effect on thatch than solid tine aeration.

Types of machines

One of the machines you can utilize in order to aerate your lawn is the use of an engine driven unit. These units have either a powerful engine that both propels the machine forward and powers the tines to punch holes into the ground. These can either be a walking unit or riding unit and can be rented in order to complete the job on your lawn. If you are within the United States the Home Depot has engine driven aeration units available for rent. If you are in the market to purchase a unit then I would suggest Ryan as your go to company on a budget.

The second type of aerator is a PTO tractor driven model. These are powered by the rear PTO of the tractor and thus do not need an engine to power them. These are usually much more powerful and more durable as they have less moving parts and are equipped to handle larger workloads. Usually finding one of these units to rent is a rarity. For applications such as large lawns needing such a unit I would recommend either finding a company to complete the job or purchasing a pull behind unit. If you insist on purchasing a PTO unit for your tractor however I suggest buying a unit from Redexim. The Redexim Verti-Drian PTO driven aerators they sell are widely considered the most durable aeration units in the industry and is my personal choice on all of my professional applications. Keep in mind however that these units are extremely expensive.

Pull behind units are used in the same applications that PTO driven aerators are but do not have the power to break up rocks nor do they have the penetration power of a PTO unit. These units can be small enough to pull with a small riding mower or large enough to need the help of a tractor. It all depends on how much you are willing to spend and what your soil is like. Obviously the harder and more compact the soil the heavier the unit you will need. If you do have harder soils such as clay a small unit may not cut it and you may be wasting money on a purchase if your small unit cannot cut it. If you cannot aerate to at least a 2" depth than the unit does not suffice for your soil type. If you have purchased a small tow behind unit and not quite getting the depth you need simply water your lawn before you aerate. This will soften the soil in order for the coring tines to penetrate deeper into the soil.

The best time of year for aeration
Depending on your climate, the best time of the year to aerate cool-season grass, such as fescue, bluegrass or rye, is in September through October or early spring once the ground has thawed from winter. Aeration during times of actively growing grass is important. For residential cool season grass aerating once per year is sufficient. Be sure never to aerate your cool season grass during the summer

months. Summer is extremely stressful on cool season grasses so minimal disruption from cultivation practices should always be avoided.

The best time to aerate warm-season grass, such as Bermuda, Paspalum, Zoysia or St. Augustine or Centipede is April-June. You can aerate warm season grasses during summer as we do as golf course superintendents but it's always best practice to avoid it. Summer aerations will have an additional drying effect on the top 2" of your soil and cause unneeded stress to your turf if you are not extremely careful and prepared. For residential warm season grass aerating once per year is sufficient but twice per year is optimal.

Preparing your lawn for aeration

The day before aeration water your lawn with a normal cycle of water. This watering will help the aerator penetrate the soil, pull out soil cores much easier and create less wear and tear on the machine. Clearly mark all hidden obstacles such as irrigation heads with marking flags or turf marking paint.

> Cool season variety (early spring):
>> Metal leaf rake your entire lawn: This will stimulate growth and clean all dead leaf material from the canopy of the lawn.

> Warm season grasses (late spring):
>> Verticut @ ¼" depth: This will remove extra thatch material from the top canopy of the lawn.

Note: You can easily create dead spots on your lawn if you aerate dry grass spots. Be sure that all spots on your lawn have received sufficient water prior to aeration but also not so wet you create ruts in your lawn from the heavy aeration machine.

Time to Aerate

Run the core aerator over the lawn in a pattern that covers the area only once. Best practice is to aerate a few passes within the outside perimeter of your lawn. This will give you a nice border to aerate in between. From there I consider strait lines to be the best way as it assures even aeration holes. Your goal is to aerate to a depth of 2.5" – 3.5" with a spacing of 2.5 - 3" between holes. Upon running the machine make sure you enlist the help of a friend of family member for the first few minutes of operation. They will be looking directly at the ground where the tines are penetrating the soil surface in order to make sure you are not peeling up large chunks of grass which can happen from a weak root zone. If an area does happen to peel, finish aeration repair the area and take mental note of its whereabouts. This can become dry very quickly and may need extra attention. If this peeling is occurring throughout your first aeration pass than raise the depth of the unit by .5" at a time until you are no longer peeling the top layer of turf.

Post aeration techniques

There are several different things that you can do here with many companies and people expressing different views on the subject. Some rake up the soil plugs and create compost piles, while others leave them on the ground and let them slowly decompose. Again no lawn is the same as the next one, it all depends on your soil tests.

With high organic matter soils I would suggest raking up and taking away the cores followed by a good sand topdressing. Low organic matter soils can be treated differently by breaking up the cores and rake or blow away the excess thatch that is left behind.

If you have opted to break up your cores the way I do this is to wait until later in the day or the day after until the soil surface and soil plugs are dry. Waiting will allow you to break up the cores easier and create less mess on top of your lawn. Chopping up the cores with your mower works well but with larger lawns consider the purchase of a baseball diamond drag mat. Attaching this to the back of a riding mower and driving around at a fast speed will add additional core busting power. This can take several passes with the mat depending on how dry the cores are. From this point you can either use a leaf blower or leaf rake to rake and dispose of any excess dead plant material developed from breaking up the cores. If you do choose this method be sure to sharpen your mower blades after. This will dull you're your mower blades fast. If your lawn is a cool season variety and need to add grass seed to weak spots in your lawn now is the time to do so. With all the cores broken up (or raked away) you now can apply your needed soil amendments as per the suggestions in your soil report. If you have yet to obtain a report I would suggest applying earthworm casting compost as per the mock up fertilizer plan we created earlier.

From here I would strongly recommend a sand topdressing. The only time I would suggest against this is if your soil is already very high in sand content and you are within the first few years of a new lawn on your property. But for most of us a yearly sand topdressing post aeration will help develop a well-drained, firm and root friendly environment for your lawn. For cool season grasses it's not 100%

needed but worth it if you want the best looking lawn in town. $\frac{1}{4}$"
per year will suffice on cool season grasses and for warm season $\frac{1}{4}$ -
$\frac{1}{2}$" is sufficient. A large pile of topdressing sand can be spread
evenly throughout the lawn with a wheelbarrow, shovels and push
broom. As a mock up example let's say your lawn is 10,000sqft of
Celebration Bermuda grass and you have just completed the aeration
and application of worm compost. You've already ordered a bulk
shipment of 14 yards of topdressing sand and is piled up and ready to
go in your driveway. As we briefly talked about earlier we know
already that 14 yards will cover your 10,000sqft lawn with a perfect
$\frac{1}{2}$" of sand. So in order to spread evenly we are just going to break
up the pile into smaller piles spread evenly across your lawn. This is
done with a shovel and wheelbarrow. Once you have exhausted the
pile and spread equally sized piles across your lawn you can simply
spread each pile uniformly around with your shovel. Once this is
done you can use your broom to make everything smooth.

As a last step I hope you've timed your fertilizer application to
coincide with your aeration. If you have done so you can now apply
your due fertilizer on top of your freshly top-dressed lawn. Once the
application of fertilizer has been completed you may now water your
lawn, and quite heavily ill add. With the holes being filled with
aggressively draining sand you will need water more than what you
are used to. Be prepared to keep a keen eye on your lawn for about a
week. It may need water daily to keep from drying out.

Verticutting

Normally I like to see a lawn verticut before an aeration so I realize this topic may be a bit off in sequence but that is for good reason. Verticutting may not be something you do every year. Especially on cool season grasses you probably never will have to verticut your lawn. On warm season grasses however I would suggest checking your thatch levels yearly to make an informed decision on if you plan to verticut at all. Verticutting yearly is going to be beneficial regardless of your decision but may not be 100% needed. As long as you maintain a thatch layer less than ½" thick than you may be able to forego a verticut for the season. It may just not be worth the time, effort and added money needed.

But I digress, let's get back to the method of verticutting. Verticutting is the act of cutting into your grass with vertical blades in order to remove thatch. Thatch is the layer of built-up plant material between the green top growth and the roots of grass plants. Thatch develops naturally as lawn grasses grow and sloughs off older plant material. Some thatch helps protect the roots, but excessive thatch prevents moisture, oxygen and nutrients from penetrating the soil. Thatch can harbor diseases and insects that feed off your lawn, so it is important to manage this layer properly with both yearly aeration and verticutting cultivation practices. I don't find it necessary to use a verticut machine if you have a cool season turf variety (with bentgrass being the exception). This method would only be paramount if you have Bentgrass, Bermudagrass, Zoysia or Paspalum. For all other varieties an annual thatching rake and aerification program will suffice.

The frequency of verticutting depends on what species of grass you have, your climate, soil type and amount of nitrogen you are applying to your lawn. If you suspect your lawn is in need of verticutting, first you will have to examine the thatch layer. You can use a small shovel to dig a hole to measure the thickness of your thatch layer. If the thatch layer measures more than ½" in depth you should prepare to verticut your lawn. The depth and spacing of the verticut should also be played with until you find the right measurement for you. Consider a depth of 0.25" and spacing of 1" to start with. Any tighter spacing than that can create quite a tender lawn for a few weeks but by all means play with the depth until you find what's right for you.

If your lawn has been neglected and your thatch layer is quite a bit thicker than ½", you may need to do this multiple times per year until you have your thatch layer under control. Warm season grasses that spread by stolons and rhizomes are quicker to build up a thatch layer. As these stolons and rhizomes build up on top of one another you can begin to feel a puffy mattress like feel when walking on your grass. This is a sure indication that your thatch is getting out of hand. If you do have a warm season grass plan on verticutting once a year in order to maintain a healthy growing lawn. Again there are several factors at play here, so periodic observation should be done in order to get the right frequency for your lawn. If you find your grass to need more verticutting than once a year than you may want to consider backing off of your yearly nitrogen rates by about ½ lb. per year.

If you have a small lawn you can get away with using a thatching rake. Not any rake will do, a thatching rake is a specific tool meant for de-thatching your lawn. To use it you simply rake in one direction with some down force. After completing the entire lawn you than can go over the lawn again in a direction perpendicular to your first direction. If your thatch layer is not severe than this second pass may not be necessary. Once you have completed your entire lawn you can use a leaf rake to rake up all the thatch and start a compost pile with it. This can then be recycled back into the lawn once the compost is fully broken down.

If your lawn is a bit larger and or your thatch is extremely thick you can rent a machine to do the job with less effort. If you are within the United States Home Depot is a good bet to rent your verticutting unit. They are not mentioned on their website so be sure to call ahead and make sure they have one available for you. Ask Home Depot to adjust the verticutting unit for you to ¼" if possible and be sure to ask what the spacing is between each blade (1" is optimal). If you are adjusting the unit yourself never go deeper than ½" below the surface. Going deeper risks damaging the blades of the verticutting unit and can tear up roots of the plant. Be sure to mark any irrigation heads, rocks or any other obstacles in your lawn with marking flags or turf paint before you start operating the machine.

Verticut in strait lines, just like you would do while mowing. After completing one direction you can than go over your lawn again in a direction perpendicular to your first direction. If your thatch is minimal this second direction may not be needed. If you would like to purchase a verticutting unit than I would recommend a product from Ryan or for heavy duty use go with Graden or Sisis. Sisis to me is a more durable and dependable unit and they also sell larger hydraulic driven choices for large lawns or commercial use. If you are unsure of completing verticutting on your own consider hiring a professional.

You can remove thatch in summer, fall and even when the lawn is dormant in winter. Though my suggestion is to verticut on the day before you aerify you lawn. Verticutting before aerifying is a common practice and a good way to rejuvenate your turf. Make sure that when you do choose to verticut and aerify your grass is actively growing. For warm season varieties make sure your grass has come out of winter dormancy (if you are in a transition zone).

PESTS

Weeds

Weeds in the lawn are a nuisance. By now you know how to maintain your lawn properly enough to minimize the encroachment of weeds but truly being organically weed free requires a lot of extra work. Without the use of pre-emergent herbicides, being completely clean of weeds is impossible. So you will either have to learn to live with them or pull them. There are of course ways of lessening weed infestation.

An overabundance of weeds in your lawn is a sign of unhealthy turf caused by improper fertilizer program or irrigation practices. There are many ways to kill weeds organically with vinegar, salt, or a torch but these methods will also kill your grass. Organic weed control isn't a perfect system, nor does it need to be. Maintaining a healthy lawn doesn't mean it needs to be weed free. You can successfully get your weeds under control by using organic methods, just get the thought of a completely weed free lawn out of your head unless you use pre-emergent herbicides. The one two punch of increasing the health of your lawn and spending a few hours a week pulling weeds will slowly get your lawn under control.

As far as preventing weeds from germinating you can try corn gluten meal. I for one have yet to try it but it's an organic pre-emergent herbicide that has a small dose of nitrogen as well. Studies show it's been shown to work well for some weeds, though contrary to any others belief it does not give total control of all weed seeds. This product is also extremely expensive. In fact if you have a larger lawn I would suggest not even considering its use. You can expect to pay close to $30.00 per 1000sqft. The least expensive brand that I have found is Espoma Organic Weed Preventer.

Prevent weeds with proper lawn care practices:
- Grow the appropriate grass for your area
- Check sprinkler heads monthly if you have an irrigation system
- Water deep and infrequent. Your goal is to water 2-4 times per week
- Mow regularly enough to not scalp your grass
- Fertilize 4-6 times annually: see fertilization section
- Aerate your soil at least once per year
- Verti-cut your lawn if your thatch is more than half an inch thick.

A list of common weeds and their underlying lawn care issue
Below I have listed some common weeds you might find within your lawn. Each weed tells a story of the conditions of your soil. Some weeds like wet and heavy soils while others like sandy dry soils. When you have successfully identified a few species of weeds these can tell you a lot about the soil conditions. When you know your soil conditions you can slowly work at your soil structure to alleviate the problems. It is important to know that many weeds can grow in many types of soil conditions, so it is important to accurately identify several types of weeds before assuming your soil is associated with any one problem. For the most part I have kept the list short and tried to leave out weeds that are known to thrive in many types of soil conditions.

More importantly, I'm not here to waste your time with weed identification. And I'm not about to waste my time or yours by trying to make a better weed identification guide. Truthfully I don't believe I have opened my weed identification books since college. Instead use the Weed Identification Guide from the University of Missouri @ https://weedid.missouri.edu/. It's easy to use and has over 400 species listed which has turned out to be enough for most all of my weed identification issues. Once you have found the weeds you are dealing with by using the Weed ID Guide, use my quick reference below to troubleshoot why you got the weeds in the first place.

Grassy weeds

- Annual bluegrass – Compacted or heavy soil, Wet or poorly drained soil, High fertility soil, Shaded soil
- Bentgrasses – Acid soil, High fertility soil
- Crabgrass– High fertility soil, Wet or poorly drained soil
- Kyllinga – Wet or poorly drained soil
- Nimblewill - Shaded soil
- Quack grass – Hardpan soil or hard crust
- Sedges – Wet or poorly drained soil
- Yellow nutsedge – Wet or poorly drained soils

Broadleaf weeds

- Black medic – Dry soil
- Bladder campion – Alkaline soil
- Broadleaf dock – Compacted or heavy soil

- Burdock – High fertility soil
- Butter print – High fertility soil
- Canada goldenrod – Wet or poorly drained soil
- Carpetweed – Previously cultivated soil
- Chickweed – Previously cultivated soil
- Chicory – High fertility soil
- Coltsfoot – Wet/poorly drained soil
- Common chickweed - Shaded soil, Wet or poorly drained soil, Compacted or heavy soil
- Creeping buttercup – Compacted or heavy soil, Wet or poorly drained soil
- Curly dock – Wet or poorly drained soil
- Dandelion – Compacted or heavy soil, High fertility soil, Previously cultivated soil
- Field mustard – Hardpan soil or hard crust
- Field peppergrass – Alkaline soil
- Goosefoot – Alkaline soil, Compacted or heavy soil, Wet or poorly drained soil
- Gromwell – Alkaline soil
- Ground ivy - Shaded soil, Wet or poorly drained soil
- Ground nut – Wet or poorly drained soil
- Hawkweeds – Acid soil
- Henbit – High fertility soil
- Horse nettle – Hardpan soil or hard crust
- Horsetail – Wet or poorly drained soil
- Jewelweed – Wet or poorly drained soil
- Joe-pye weed – Wet or poorly drained soil
- Knapweeds – Acid soil

- Knotweed – Compacted or heavy soil
- Lady's-thumb – Acid soil, Wet or poorly drained soil
- Lamb's-quarters – Previously cultivated soil, High fertility soil
- Lance-leaved goldenrod – Wet or poorly drained soil
- Mallow– High fertility soil
- Meadow pink – Wet or poorly drained soil
- Morning-glory – Hardpan soil or hard crust
- Mosses – Wet or poorly drained soil
- Mouse-ear chickweed – Compacted or heavy soil, Shaded soil, Wet or poorly drained soil
- Pennsylvania smartweed – Wet or poorly drained soil
- Pennycress – Hardpan soil or hard crust
- Pigweeds – High fertility soil, Previously cultivated soil
- Pineapple weed – Hardpan soil or hard crust
- Plantain – Previously cultivated soil, Acid soil, Compacted or heavy soil, Low fertility soil
- Pokeweed – High fertility soil
- Potato vine – Dry soil
- Prostrate knotweed – Acid soil
- Prostrate spurge – Compacted or heavy soil
- Purslane – High fertility soil, Previously cultivated soil
- Queen Anne's lace – High fertility soil
- Ragweed – Previously cultivated soil
- Red sorrel – Dry soil, Low fertility soil
- Rough cinquefoil – Acid soil, Dry soil
- Sheep sorrel – Wet or poorly drained soil
- Silvery cinquefoil – Acid soil, Wet or poorly drained soil
- Sorrel – Acid soil

- Sow thistle – Acid soil
- Sweet flag – Wet or poorly drained soil
- Tall buttercup – Wet or poorly drained soil
- True chamomile – Alkaline soil
- Violets – Wet or poorly drained soil, Shaded soil
- Virginia pepperweed – Dry soil
- White clover – Low fertility soil
- Wild garlic – Compacted or heavy soil
- Wild strawberries – Acid soil
- Yarrow – Dry soil
- Yellow woodsorrel – High fertility soil

Diseases

For the most part diseases can be avoided on lawns with proper cultural practices such as watering techniques, mowing and fertilization. To ensure your grass remains disease free please follow the guidelines for each in previous chapters. If diseases appear adjust your fertilization slightly by the recommendations for the disease you have. Creating unfavorable conditions for diseases is always a good practice. If you do have an uncontrollable outbreak I do recommend the use of an organic fungicide such as Actinovate Lawn and Garden Fungicide until you have the problem under control. NOTE: This fungicide does need a liquid applicator just like the ones I have mentioned within the fertilization chapter. Be sure to clean this applicator thoroughly after each use and follow the instructions on the bag of fungicide in order to get the correct dosage your lawn needs.

For the most part pictures of diseases aren't very beneficial. It's hard to detect the difference of certain diseases just by looking at them alone and in fact a lot of the pictures that are out there on the internet are incorrect identifications. Personally when I have a tough disease to identify I just end up sending away a sample of the grass and soil to a lab I use that correctly identify the disease. For example, fusarium can look just like dollar spot and soil borne diseases can be almost impossible to identify by a simple picture alone. It's better to know the conditions favorable to spawn the disease to narrow down the type you are dealing with. A lot of times diseases can be remedied with simple changes to your watering and nutrients.

If you unfortunately do come across a tough identification or severe outbreak we can work through a more detailed process on how to get it under control or get your soil sample to the correct laboratory for examination. For more information go to the back of the book to the Beyond the Book chapter.

Fairy Ring - All grasses

Symptoms: A dark green circle of turf develops (can be small or very large) or semicircle in moist turf. Depending on the stage of the disease mushrooms might or might not be present. Older rings will show an area of brown, dying grass that occur just behind the dark green band.

Conditions favoring disease: Soils high in thatch or undecomposed organic matter containing wood.

Prevention: The best prevention is to maintain a healthy lawn by completing annual aerations and continually applying organic fertilizers.   This will increase microbial activity which will ward off the disease.

Treatment: This disease is by far the toughest I have had to get rid of and is a nuisance on many golf courses. Even chemical treatments of the disease do not guarantee control. Fairy ring can be eliminated by removing the turf and root zone with the soil containing the fungal mass. This should be replaced with fresh soil mixed with a bit of compost to help build up beneficial soil microbe populations. I would suggest however to keep a close eye on the fungus over the course of 18 months after implementing the organic fertilizers and principles talked about in this book. There is a good chance that the newly energized microbial activity will fight off the disease to acceptable levels.

Large Patch or brown patch – All grasses

Symptoms: First appears as small, irregular brown patches or rings that can enlarge to many feet in diameter. The centers of the rings will appear thin and weak. The color of the interior of the ring will look slightly off or brownish yellow in appearance. The grass blades will pull out easily from soil due to the roots and stolon's becoming rotten.

Conditions favoring disease: Excess thatch, wet soil and cool temperatures (60°–80°F).

Prevention: Pruning trees around your lawn will help with air movement and sunlight for your lawn. Keeping a close eye on your irrigation system and or looking for wet spots after a rain can be helpful. Wet spots after a rain will indicate areas needing drainage. Wet spots after an irrigation cycle can be alleviated with an adjustment to your irrigation run times.

Chemical treatment: The best treatment is a sound prevention program. But for an organic solution to eliminating a present active disease I would try and organic fungicide containing beneficial organisms such as Actinovate.

Rhizoctonia blight - Bluegrass, fescues, ryegrasses

Symptoms: Very similar to brown or large patch.

Conditions favoring disease: Excess thatch, excess nitrogen and high temperatures.

Prevention: Pruning trees around your lawn will help with air movement and sunlight. Keeping a close eye on your irrigation system and looking for wet spots after a rain. Wet spots after a rain will indicate areas needing drainage. Wet spots after an irrigation cycle can be alleviated with an adjustment to your irrigation. Be sure to aerate annually and you are not applying too much nitrogen.

Treatment: The best treatment is prevention. But for an organic solution to eliminating a present active disease I would try annual or bi-annual applications of a biological fungicide.

Dollar spot – all grasses

Symptoms: Small, circular spots from 1–5inch in diameter; spots can come together to form large brown turf spots. The leaves appear water soaked & brown, often exhibiting a reddish band across the leaf. If you wake up early in the morning to fine white threads (mycelium) within the affected areas than this is a sure indication of the disease.

It is worth noting that some insects can also form similar looking cobwebbing. It could either be harmless turf spiders or harmful sod webworms. Be sure to inspect the grass underneath the webbing to diagnose the culprit.

Conditions favoring disease: Heavy dew, moderate temperatures (60°–80°F) high air humidity and low nitrogen can all cause dollar spot.

Prevention: Fertilize adequately with organic nitrogen sources. Reduce your thatch layer if it is greater than ½". Water deeply and infrequently. Water in the early morning hours in order to keep dew from setting in. Yearly compost top dressing after aeration can also suppress the disease. If you notice dew setting in during the morning you may water your grass lightly just to knock the dew off the blade.

Treatment: Dollar spot is rarely serious enough on home lawns to warrant the use of an organic fungicide. The best treatment is a sound prevention program. Consider raising your nitrogen levels by 1/2lb per year.

Rusts - all grasses

Symptoms: Weak colored turf with rust colored growths.

Conditions favoring disease: Low nitrogen and extended periods of dew or soil wetness.

Prevention: Proper irrigation and fertilization.

Treatment: Rusts often indicate low levels of nitrogen. Consider applying fertilizer if it is time to do so. Also mow regularly and remove clippings to reduce number of spores if lawn is infected. If in 1-2 weeks the problem still persists you may try using an organic fungicide such as Actinovate for a kick in the pants.

Slime molds - all grasses

Symptoms: Slimy paste like material that covers the leaf blades that quickly changes to a soot like material in the afternoon. The color can vary drastically among species from blue, red, white, yellow or tan.

Conditions favoring disease: They are most prevalent following prolonged periods of leaf wetness and may be observed from late spring to late fall. Shade can also be a culprit.

Prevention: Areas with poor drainage and heavy thatch also may enhance disease pressure.

Treatment: This is not a serious disease but indirectly can shade out your grass causing yellowing. If slime molds occur you can simply sweep them off with a rake, broom or garden hose during the afternoon hours.

Powdery mildews – Kentucky bluegrass, fescues

Symptoms: Affected turf has a white or light gray appearance. White spores may cover the entire leaf blade.

Conditions favoring disease: Shady, cool, cloudy conditions. First outbreaks can occur under high humidity and nitrogen situations.

Prevention: Shade-tolerant Kentucky bluegrass varieties tend to be less susceptible to powdery mildew. Over seeding shaded areas with these varieties will reduce powdery mildew outbreaks. Improving air circulation by carefully pruning trees and shrubs also will help limit mildew development. Consider lowering nitrogen levels by 1/2lb per year.

Treatment: If the appearance of mildew-infected turf is absolutely intolerable, organic fungicides may be applied for effective control.

Red Thread – Bent grasses, Bermuda grasses bluegrasses, fescues, ryegrasses

Symptoms: Look for red threads that occur in small patches. These threads can bind leaves together.

Conditions favoring disease: Low nitrogen, mild air conditions, extended periods of dew.

Prevention: Proper deep and infrequent irrigation and fertilization can reduce the problem. Also adequate nitrogen usually can prevent this disease from occurring. Provide adequate air circulation and reduce shading by pruning or removing trees in and around your lawn.

Treatment: Fungicides are rarely warranted except in severe cases. The best treatment is a sound fertilizer/watering/cultivation program.

Fusarium - All grasses

Symptoms: Often referred to as "frog's eye" the small, circular patterns are grey and can vary in size. Some plants in center can survive which gives a frog-eye appearance. A good indicator is that dead foliage will appear bleached out.

Conditions favoring disease: Hot temperatures, drought-stress, and in full sun.

Prevention: Water deep and infrequent. Keep a sound organic fertility program. Mow at a higher height of cut and consider a verticut or aerification to reduce thatch.

Treatment: The best treatment is a sound prevention program. But for an organic solution to eliminating a present active disease I would try and organic fungicide.

Grey leaf spot - Fescues, kikuyu grass, ryegrasses, St. Augustine grass

Symptoms: Irregular patches of turf that have bleached spots with dark margins on leaves.

Conditions favoring disease: Hot temperatures, high fertility, high humidity or rainfall.

Prevention: Irrigate deep and infrequently. Don't over fertilize your turf. If this disease is a regular problem for you, lower your annual nitrogen by 1/2lb. Reduce shading and increase air movement by pruning or removing trees.

Treatment: Fungicides are available, but a sound prevention program is more practical. Actinovate or a similar biological fungicide can be used.

Snow mold - annual bluegrass, bluegrasses, fescues, ryegrasses, zoysia

Symptoms: Pink threads can be seen early in the morning. These threads will occur in patches of 1–2 inches that can enlarge over time. Leaves first water soaked then reddish brown.

Conditions favoring disease: Cool temperatures (40°–65°F), wet conditions with high nitrogen applications in fall.

Prevention: reduce shade by pruning or removing trees, aerate once a season and install drainage where needed. Water deep/infrequently and avoid excess nitrogen especially in fall. If this is a yearly problem avoid any nitrogen in the fall months. Find an organic source of potassium for the fall application such as sunflower hull seed ash.

Treatment: Microbial fungicides applied in the fall and spring will help ward off the disease. Once the turf dries out the affected areas should cure quite quickly. Consider an early aerification and application of grass seed to help recover at a faster pace.

Leaf spot - All grasses

Symptoms: Circular to elongated brownish spots with brown centers and dark brown or purple borders on leaf blades, sheaths, and stems. Crowns and roots frequently have a dark brown rot.

Conditions favoring disease: For cool season grasses: warm temperatures (70°–90°F). For warm season grasses: cool temperatures (60°–70°F). Humid conditions also favor development.

Prevention: Reduce shade by pruning or removing trees in the lawn. Improve soil aeration and water drainage. Avoid dry spots, too much nitrogen and maintain as high a cutting height as possible.

Chemical treatment: Fungicides available but often not warranted

Pythium - All grasses

Symptoms: Grease like spots that look like blackened leaf blades. These blades will quickly die and turn to a reddish brown.

Conditions favoring disease: Low spots that remain wet with warm temperatures (80°–95°F daytime and greater than 68F night time).

Prevention: Avoid high nitrogen during the summer months. Keep a close eye out for wet spots on your lawn. Do not mow if ground is overly wet during times of high temperatures.

Chemical treatment: Fungicides available but primarily prevented by cultural practices

Summer patch - Bluegrasses, fine fescues

Symptoms: Circular, yellow or tan areas of dead and dying plants up to 1 foot in diameter. The affected area can have healthy grass within the circle.

Conditions favoring disease: High temperatures (greater than 85°), low mowing heights and excess soil moisture

Prevention: Aerate soil and apply a slow-release organic nitrogen. Consider installing drainage if problem persists. Water deep and infrequently. Don't mow too low, and control thatch by yearly verticutting and aerating. Complete a soil test to ensure that your soil pH is 7 or lower.

Treatment: This is a hard fungus to treat after symptoms show. In areas where summer patch is frequent, begin biological fungicide applications in the spring. Aerate, apply compost and biological fungicide if outbreak occurs.

Spring dead spot - Bermudagrass, Seashore paspalum , zoysia

Symptoms: Areas of dead grass 6–12 inches in diameter appear in spring when growth resumes. I have observed spring dead spot in the fall as well during wet weather. Typically never active on newly seeded or sodded lawns.

Conditions favoring disease: Affects dormant plants and plants just coming out of winter dormancy. Low soil temps of 65°F.

Prevention: Remove dead grass with thatching rake. Maintain adequate fertility through the season and keep nitrogen low or absent in the fall. Water deep and infrequently.

Chemical treatment: Fungicides available but primarily prevented by cultural practices

Insects

Much like diseases most insect problems can be prevented just by implementing correct cultural practices just like the ones described in this guide. If insects are a yearly problem for your lawn I would suggest the preventative treatments of parasitic nematodes 3 times a year and to always have neem oil on hand for outbreaks. Between both products you can control most insects are both safe and will not kill beneficial insects. If ants are a concern always keep a bottle of orange oil around the house.

It is also a good idea to introduce beneficial insects into your lawn prior to outbreaks of pest insects. These beneficial insects include lady beetles, praying mantis and mealybug destroyers. Most of these can be found quite readily through Amazon or other vendors.

NOTE: Some of these products do require a simple liquid applicator like the echo 3 gallon or Gilmour I mentioned earlier in the liquid calibration section. This applicator can also be used for application of liquid organic fertilizers as well. Be sure to clean this applicator thoroughly after each use and follow the instructions on the bag of fungicide in order to get the correct dosage your lawn needs.

Armyworms, Webworms & Cutworms

Size: 2- 34 mm depending on life stage

Symptoms: Bare or Ragged Patches that appear to be chewed. If armyworms are present, you'll be able to see the pests eating your grass. Worms can be found throughout the day but easier to spot in the morning hours.

Prevention: It's hard to prevent outbreaks of worms. If you have annual worm infestations consider reseeding with endophyte-enhanced grass varieties. Or using parasitic nematodes before your next outbreak occurs.

Treatment: *Bacillus thuringiensis* (BT) - effective when the larvae are small. Parasitic nematodes can be applied up to 3 times per year. Insecticidal soaps work but only effective on contact with caterpillar so make sure to drench the area. Neem extracts work as a growth and feeding regulator and work best when applied applied to small larvae.

Ants

Size: 2-6 mm (fire ant) 6-12mm (carpenter ant)

Symptoms: Mounds of sand or dirt within your lawn.

Prevention: Consider trying to discover their food source. In many cases ants can be a helpful indicator of other pests like armyworms/cutworms. Your ant populations may very well be helping keep other pests at bay. On the other hand ants do have a tendency to harvest aphids and use their honeydew as a food source. They will protect aphids from natural predators and quickly increase their population. The presence of a large population of aphids may also be harmful to your lawn and surrounding plants.

Treatment: Orange oil – This product kills on contact action so it is important to fully drench the mound.

Japanese beetles

Size: Depending on age (grubs) 15mm (adult)

Symptoms: White grub Larvae feed on roots, causing symptoms that first appear to look like dry grass. Birds and raccoons tear up the grass attempting to get to the grubs. **Note:** Identification of Japanese beetle grubs is done by looking at their underside tail hairs. Hairs will form in the shape of a V pointing to their stomach. You may need to purchase a loupe if it is hard to tell.

Prevention: Some people think a good indicator of your Japanese beetle populations is the use of traps. However several university studies prove that the use of traps attract more Japanese beetles to your property. If Japanese beetles are an annual nuisance in your lawn the regular use of parasitic nematodes would offer the best prevention for the pests.

Treatment: Milky spore – Some people swear by it, but this product has shown extremely unreliable results. Parasitic nematodes can be applied up to 3 times per year. It is important to. Read the label carefully and follow its directions on applications.

European chafers & other beetles

Size: 20-25mm (grubs) 15mm (adult)

Symptoms: Just like Japanese beetles there are some other beetle species that feed on lawns in the larvae stage such as European chafers, masked chafers & green June beetles. When larvae feed on roots they cause symptoms that first appear to look like dry grass. Birds and rodent damage to your lawn is an early indication of outbreak.

Prevention: Similarly to Japanese beetle prevention, if beetles are an annual nuisance in your lawn the regular use of parasitic nematodes would offer the best prevention for the pests. Beetle traps that are commonly sold will only attract Japanese beetles, and not European chafer.

Treatment: Parasitic nematodes can be applied up to 3 times per year. It is important to. Read the label carefully and follow its directions on applications.

Mole crickets

Size: 30-35mm

Symptoms: Mole crickets tunnel underground to eat roots. Tunnels can clearly be seen and grass that has been damaged begins to thin and then disappear.

Prevention: Early detection of mole crickets is the key to control. Mix one ounce of dishwashing detergent in a gallon of water. Keep soaking the soil making the insect loose his oxygen source. If you have mole crickets they should come to the surface within a few minutes. If mole crickets are an annual problem for you. Consider applying parasitic nematodes in early spring through summer for control.

Treatment: Parasitic nematodes can be applied up to 3 times per year. It is important to. Read the label carefully and follow its directions on applications.

Annual bluegrass weevil

Size: 1-4mm (grub) 3mm (adult)

Symptoms: Despite its name the annual bluegrass weevil can also effect bluegrass and ryegrass varieties. Look for growing areas of yellow and brown patches. Since this damage can look similar to that of other insects and diseases a quick way to test if you have annual bluegrass weevil is to do a tug test. Pulling lightly on affected grass will pull up stems of your grass that have been weakened by the weevil. Upon closer inspection with a loupe you may notice the excrement left behind in their feeding.

Prevention: Removal of leaf litter and downed pine needles before winter can help deter adults from over wintering on your property.

Treatment: Again Parasitic nematodes are the go to organic cure for bluegrass weevil. These can be applied up to 3 times per year (spring, summer and fall). Remember that parasitic nematodes are a living creature and certain cares have to be made while applying this product. Read the label carefully and follow its directions on applications.

Chinch bugs

Size: 2mm

Symptoms: Resembles grass suffering from drought. This can easily be ruled out by taking a shovel, dig a few inches down to see if your soil is moist. If it is moist, closely inspect the grass inside the affected area and the area on the outer edge of the affected area. Chinch bug damage first starts with blades wilting, then turning yellowish-brown, then dry out and die. Chinch bugs are sometimes hard to find just by looking around, if you cannot find them then we can use the tin can method. Cut out both ends of a tin can, making a tube. Push one end of your tube into the ground about an inch. Then pour water into the can and keep it filled for 10 minutes. If you have chinch bugs, they'll start floating up to the top.

Prevention: Chinch bugs prefer lawns high in thatch and organic debris such as un-mulched or bagged leaves. Using the proper mowing and de-thatching practices found in this e-book will minimize the effect chinch bugs have on your turf. Endophyte enhanced grasses can also offer resistance to chinch bugs.

Treatment: Again Parasitic nematodes are the go to organic cure for chinch bugs. These can be applied up to 3 times per year (spring, summer and fall). Remember that parasitic nematodes are a living creature and certain cares have to be made while applying this product. Read the label carefully and follow its directions on applications.

Thrips

Size: 0.5 to 14 mm

Symptoms: Brown or a mottled silver dried grass. The thrips themselves are actually very small (5mm or less) and hard to spot. Their fecal matter will appear as black sooty spots on leaves.

Prevention: Studies show that dry grass has more severe infestations than grass that has insufficient moisture. Check your lawn regularly for dry spots. If you have automatic irrigation you should adjust your times accordingly to accommodate for these spots. If you do not have an irrigation system a simple hand watering with a hose of all your dry spots will suffice.

Treatment: Parasitic nematodes work really well for thrips. These can be applied up to 3 times per year (spring, summer and fall). Remember that parasitic nematodes are a living creature and certain cares have to be made while applying this product. Read the label carefully and follow its directions on applications.

Aphids

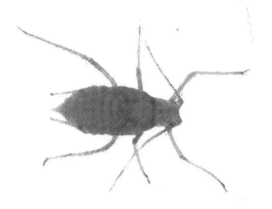

Size: 2-5mm

Symptoms: Damage is usually noticed as large round discolored patches. Inspect grass blades with a loupe on the outer edges of the affected area. If aphids are present they will show up normally on the upper part of the leaf blade.

Prevention: Removal of organic debris from your lawn is the best prevention against aphids.

Treatment: Neem oil kills aphids quickly. If you spray this on your lawn make sure you apply enough to sufficiently cover the entire grass blade.

Introducing lady beetles into your lawn works great. Keep them refrigerated and make sure you do not release them during the heat of the day. Releasing them at dusk will give you the best chance of success.

Introducing Mealybug destroyers (*Cryptolaemus montrouzieri*) can be purchased for reasonable prices on Amazon. These insects are a natural predator of mealybugs and aphids.

Introducing praying mantis can also be helpful though it may prove to be difficult after an outbreak has begun.

Fleas

Size: 1.5 to 3.3 mm

Symptoms: Small red bites on legs or ankles. If you notice your pet regularly getting fleas then it may be a good idea to treat your lawn.

Prevention/Treatment: Parasitic nematodes have shown in studies to work extremely well on lawn fleas. These can be applied up to 3 times per year (spring, summer and fall). Remember that parasitic nematodes are a living creature and certain cares have to be made while applying this product. Read the label carefully and follow its directions on applications.

Mealybugs

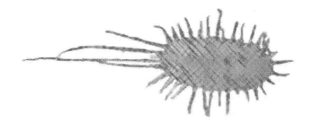

Size: 1-4mm

Symptoms: Mealybugs suck the juices from grass which cause discoloration and wilting. This damage thins the turf and causes stunted growth. Heavy mealybug pressure can cause white secretions on the plants, which promotes the growth of molds.

Prevention: The best prevention is a sound turf care plan and weekly scouting of your lawn. Keeping a close eye on your turf grass goes a long way. Inspection is your most valuable weapon against insects like mealybugs. With a quick identification of an outbreak mealybugs can easily be controlled.

Treatment: Neem oil kills mealybugs fairly rapidly if you spray this on your lawn make sure you apply enough to sufficiently cover the entire grass blade.

Introducing mealybug destroyers (*Cryptolaemus montrouzieri*). These insects are a natural predator of mealybugs and aphids. Each insect can eat up to 250 mealybug larvae per day.

Introducing lady beetles into your lawn works great. Keep them refrigerated and make sure you do not release them during the heat of the day. Releasing them at dusk will give you the best chance of success.

Mites

Size: <1mm

Symptoms: Damage is characterized by general lack of plant health and a silvery or pale yellow discoloration on leaves. As damage progresses, grass will gradually turn yellow, dry out and die. With the help of a loupe (easily found on amazon) mites can be observed within thatch or grass blades.

Prevention: Keep your lawn clean of debris such as leaves, pine needles and other things that may have fallen on your turf.

Treatment: Neem oil kills mites quickly if you spray this on your lawn make sure you apply enough to sufficiently cover the entire grass blade.

European crane fly

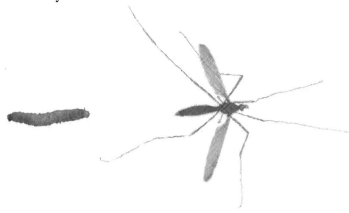

Size: 2.5 - 3.8 cm (grubs) 2.5 - 3.0 cm (adults)

Symptoms: Appearing in spring and fall. Heavy insect pressure will appear in a brownish paste on your lawn. Normal damage appears in patches that will eventually grow together and spread.
Dig into your soil and look for brownish-grey larvae about 1 inch long. If your grass is healthy and you see crane larvae not doing any damage don't bother treating them. However it's my suggestion that if you are seeing a lot of larvae, it's a good practice to wipe them out even if your grass appears healthy.

Prevention: Deep and infrequent watering can be a great prevention against crane fly. The eggs need adequate moisture within the top inch to be able to hatch. Keeping that top layer dry through proper irrigation practices can limit the populations drastically.

Treatment: Parasitic nematodes. These can be applied up to 3 times per year (spring, summer and fall). Remember that parasitic nematodes are a living creature and certain cares have to be made while applying this product. Read the label carefully and follow its directions on applications.

Nematodes

Nematodes are a microscopic organisms that feed on roots and rhizomes within your soil. Nematode problems for homeowners or landscapers is extremely rare and normally only addressed on golf course putting greens mown at very low heights. Diagnosis of nematode populations takes the use of a soil lab specifically designed for identification of nematodes. The problem with Nematodes are that their symptoms look a lot like symptoms caused from other problems. Typically nematode problems look like dry grass or grass that is very weak in nutrients. Before claiming you have a nematode outbreak lets take some time and walkthrough the common problems wrongfully identified as nematodes.

Check soil moisture:

Wet soil: If you have had little to no rain in the past few weeks and you have very wet areas in your lawn you may need to adjust irrigation runtimes or lower the cycles per week. Also check all valves to make sure no valves are sticking on during the night. To do this you will need to manually run your valves through your irrigation timer for a few minutes. If they shut off then they are fine. If you do change runtime values or lower the cycles per week document the health of your lawn with weekly pictures.

Dry soil: Check to make sure all your irrigation zones are running correctly by manually running your valves through the irrigation timer. While the valve is running make sure all the sprinkler heads are adjusted correctly. If you have spotted a head out of adjustment or a valve not responding with the timer this is easily fixed. See the watering section within this book.

Check fertility:
It's a best practice to check your soil nutrients at least once every 2 years. If you're due for a fertilizer application or due for a soil testing its best to do so now. Do not apply a fertilizer unless you are due to apply one based from the fertilizer plan section of this book. Applying extra fertilizer can magnify the problem if it is not a nematode outbreak or cause other problems.

Review the pests section:
You could be dealing with a Rhizoctonia (root born) disease or an insect problem. It's important you review the pest section extensively to rule out any of these scenarios.

Ok you've went through and eliminated the obvious, but Before I walk you through the practice here's a little back story....When taking my job here in South Florida my course was the Nematode capital of Florida. The previous superintendent had applied many chemical treatments to no avail. Nematode counts were higher than I have actually ever heard of. So high that golf course superintendents in the area were actually coming down to talk to him about what he was doing to help battle the nematodes. It was essentially a testing ground for synthetic chemicals.

Year after year he and his team applied harmful chemicals to the soil in an attempt to kill the nematode populations. The only results came from short declines in nematode populations then soon after spikes in nematode populations. What was happening is the chemicals where essentially nuking the soil and killing nematodes and beneficial microorganisms all at once. Without many beneficial microbes within the soil the nematodes quickly repopulated and took over again. It was a nonstop cycle of peaks and valleys of control and then outbreaks. The greens on the golf course were some of the worst I have ever seen.

In order to combat the problem I applied no chemicals and only beneficial microbes and organic products. Within 6 months we had taken outrageous populations down to almost a 0 count as stated in our nematode essays. One of the major influences to the nematode population was applying powdered crab shell, granular molasses and worm compost tea right after your annual aerification. The science behind it is that the chitin found in crab shell cell walls is the same chitin which makes up the outer cell walls of nematodes. Once an application of crab shell is made microbes begin feeding and breaking down the crab shell. The molasses acts as a fast acting boost to the microbes enhancing their repopulation rates. Once the overpopulated microbes have eaten all the crab shell they will then frantically look for other chitin sources in the area. Nematodes become their next target.

In addition to the crab shell and molasses I spray my greens with a product called Bio Amp. Bio Amp is essentially beneficial microbes in a dried state that become activated over a 24hr period in the company's machine they have created. The microbes in Bio Amp are actually intended to clean drains and sewer systems but also work extremely well at breaking down nasty materials within your soil which create more poor space and air within your soil structure. This much needed air then helps all other microbes within the soil work more efficiently. Lastly applications of fish hydrosolate, and a proprietary organic Geranium oil blend I use on my golf courses will also play backup roles in helping soil microbes combat nematodes.

BEYOND THE BOOK

It doesn't need to stop here

Need further help with your professional lawn service? Are you a homeowner looking for more of a personal training session? Perhaps you would like to get ahold of professional grade organic products or have very specific problems?

I get it, it's impossible to write a book and cover the endless amounts of problems or scenarios that can happen with your lawn. Simply visit definitiveguidetoorganiclawncare.com and find out more on how I can help. As a valued purchaser of my book you are invited to grab a free pdf copy of any updated book versions, bring questions, get product information, or find out how to receive soil testing and recommendations completed by me Daniel Stover.

Alternatively you can also find me as a certified professional on justanswer.com. As a lawn care professional on their team you can simply direct your questions to me and I will answer them as soon as possible.

Lastly I want to thank you for purchasing my Definitive Guide to Organic Lawn care. If you enjoyed this guide or want to let me know what's lacking, I'd love to read your review. Your feedback is exactly what I need to help make this book as good as it can be. To leave me a review head back to Amazon and let me know what you think. I look forward to hearing from you.

12764433R10113